THE WHISKY TRAILS

A traveller's guide to Scotch whisky

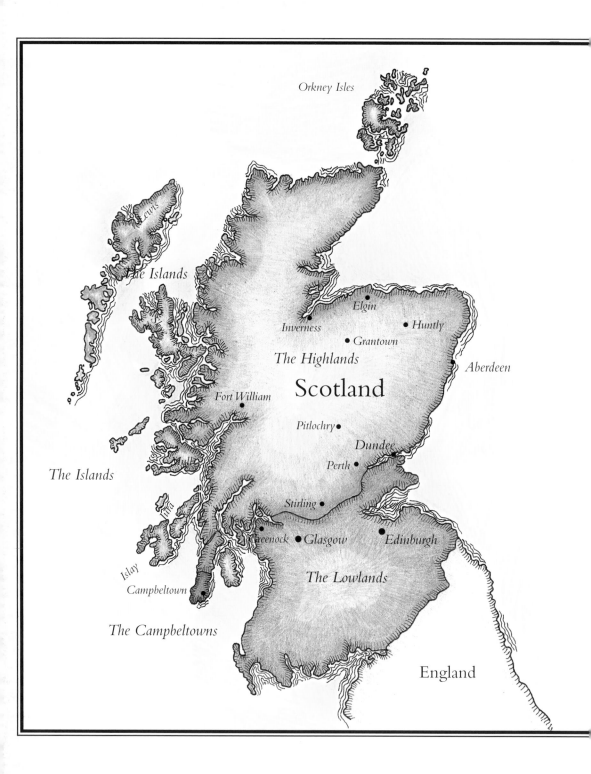

Orkney Isles

Lewis

The Islands

The Highlands

Elgin

Inverness • • Huntly

• Grantown

Aberdeen

Scotland

Fort William

Pitlochry •

Dundee

Perth •

The Islands

Stirling •

Jura

Greenock • Glasgow • Edinburgh

Islay

Campbeltown

The Lowlands

The Campbeltowns

England

THE
WHISKY
TRAILS

A traveller's guide to Scotch whisky

Gordon Brown

Foreword by **Sir Kingsley Amis**

Acknowledgements

My thanks go to everyone at the distillery companies and Scottish Tourist Board offices who kindly supplied me with up-to-date information; and to trail-walker Geoff Armitage of Dufftown.

I am especially grateful to Neil McKerrow and Victoria James of Glenmorangie; Jim Turle of Glengoyne; Richard Patterson and Moyra Peffer of Whyte & Mackay; Brian Morrison and Jim McColl of Morrison Bowmore; Nicholas Morgan of United Distillers Archive; and Matthew Gloag at Highland Distilleries – all of whom gave me access to, or data from, ongoing research programmes they are conducting not only into their respective distilleries but also into the wider social and historical contexts in which they have functioned. I congratulate these firms warmly for the fantastic heritage work they are doing.

Revised edition first published 1997 by Prion Books Ltd.,
32-34 Gordon House Road,
London NW5 1LP

Reprinted 1998

Text copyright © Gordon Brown 1993
Copyright © Prion Books Limited 1993, 1997

A catalogue record for this book is available from The British Library.

ISBN 1-85375-227-4

10 9 8 7 6 5 4 3 2

Printed and bound by Kyodo in Singapore

Contents

Foreword to the First Edition

To me, 'Scotch whisky' means malt whisky first and foremost. The other type, blended whisky, I drink chiefly when no malt is available. I could, I promise you, be endlessly learned about the different methods of manufacture, go into the history of the thing, etc., but I leave that to others. I address my brief remarks here to malt drinkers, actual or potential.

I prefer malt Scotch not only to blended Scotch, but with rare exceptions to all other spirits. Gin is good for a change, in a Dry Martini cocktail, on a hot day with ginger beer, at other times with ice, lemon and a little water but, please, never with tonic, that vile additive. Rum you need in a Planter's Punch. Vodka will make you drunk if you can swallow enough of it. Brandy doesn't agree with some people, including me. I sometimes tolerate other whiskies, or whiskeys, but only in their place. My whisky trail leads straight to Scotland, preferably the Highlands.

It would be a pity if any inquiring drinker were to be put off Scotch malt whisky by its supposedly high price. True, the stuff costs a little more than a standard blend like Bell's or Teacher's, but the difference in cost at an off-licence between an excellent malt like The Glenlivet and a classy blend like Chivas Regal is a matter of pence only. To put it another way, drinking the world's finest wines at all times would soon bankrupt the ordinary customer. No doubt many of the world's finest beers never leave their country of origin. But to have the world's finest spirit in my glass whenever I fancy is cheap in comparison, and easy.

Brandy, more especially cognac, is malt's only serious competitor. Most of those who can drink it without physical harm will soon encounter financial damage if they venture beyond the everyday price-range. At my off-licence again, a common or garden 3-star brandy just undercuts a good malt, but serious cognacs start with Rémy Martin VSOP at £25 or more, and those who go much further will be asked to fork out 80-something pounds for a bottle of Hennessy XO – a splendid drink, as I remember, but four times as good as The Glenlivet? Hardly.

From a spectrum of styles and flavours much wider than cognac offers, I with many others nominate The Macallan as my favourite malt. It's also my daily malt – I keep a stock in the house and it seems to have found its way to both my club and my local. When I step outside that circuit I sometimes have to drink other malts, Highland Park or Talisker for preference, but for me nothing really compares with Macallan 10-year-old at 40% alcohol. I stress the last phrases. Older, stronger and pricier versions exist, but to my taste they're less good, and perhaps classy malts in general are to be treated with reserve.

I try to hold to the belief that everybody is the arbiter of his or her own taste. That means in theory that you could put claret or cider vinegar into your malt without bothering me, but I must admit I turned a hair or two when my daughter-in-law, normally a well-behaved person, asked me (unsuccessfully) for ice in her Macallan. Only water should be put into a malt whisky, for it objects to being mixed with anything else, except more of itself. But some water must go in if the full

aroma and flavour are to be liberated. Tastes legitimately differ here somewhat, but my vote is for a little less than the amount of whisky, say forty-sixty.

And what water should it be? In the mind of God, that Scottish water with which that particular whisky has been made, but as things are try Evian or Volvic, even London tapwater after it has flowed for a minute or two; Glasgow tapwater is excellent. Tread carefully, because we are talking about possible accompaniments to the best drink in the world.

Sir Kingsley Amis, 1993

P u b l i s h e r s' N o t e

This revised edition was completed with the direct help of the distilleries and companies of the Scotch Whisky industry.

Gordon Brown died in November 1994, much mourned by the industry he did so much to promote.

Prion, 1997

Introduction

Anyone travelling around Scotland cannot fail frequently to encounter the whiskies for which the country is celebrated and the distilleries that produce them. No two malt whiskies are alike although family likenesses in style, flavour and aroma is easy to recognise. Similarly, a visit to one distillery gives only an inkling of what there is to know about these beautiful buildings and the part they have played in the life of the Scottish nation.

This book profiles most of the distilleries that can be visited or viewed from outside, and arranges them in a network of Whisky Trails which run the length and breadth of the country. It is equally possible to construct your own Whisky Trails by linking up the distilleries and associated places of interest that most appeal to you.

Each profile tells briefly of the distillery's history, any unique or distinctive aspects, the nature of the whisky it produces, details regarding possible visits to the

Above: The Cluanie Inn, in Glen Shiel, on the West Coast and Islands trail, is surrounded by peat moor. Some distilleries still burn peat, which gives the spirit its distinctive flavour.

distillery, and places of interest nearby. I hope your curiosity is frequently aroused by what you read in this book, and fully satisfied by what you see – and taste – on the Trails.

The Scotch whisky industry is a hospitable one and visitors to distilleries have traditionally been made welcome with advance notice and if phases of production released a staff member to act as guide.

All the information about distilleries, opening times, shops and reception centres was correct at the time of going to press. Some changes may always occur, however, and it is advisable to check on arrival.

Single-track roads

In visiting some of the more remote distilleries, you will come across the Scottish phenomenon of single-track roads with passing places. These are the legacy of successive governments which have declined to make the money available to pay for even modest two-lane roads. Passing places are just that – very short stretches of wider roadway where there is room for cars going in opposite directions to pass each other; they are not lay-bys so please do not park in them.

Skilfully used, you do not even have to stop your car. Both drivers approaching a passing place can see the marker-posts ahead so if you slow down enough to meet the other car at the spot you can usually pass each other in low second gear. Don't try to squeeze past on the open stretches away from the passing places – local drivers quite correctly use the entire width of the road and you could endanger both cars by forcing the other driver into an unexpected *fait accompli*.

The History of Scotch Whisky

The original Scotch whisky was malt whisky – often big, soupy, strong and smoky from the peat-fuelled fires used to dry the malt. Batches from a single still could vary, styles from one village to another would always vary.

Whisky was as intrinsic a part of Gaelic life as bread and had a surprising range of invaluable applications. It kept out the cold, set up the traveller for his journey and soothed him when it was over, punctuated social meetings and sealed business discussions. The scope beyond its being a mere accompaniment to other things was extraordinary. Whisky tempered fever, acted as an anaesthetic, especially in childbirth, and disinfected sword-cuts. It was even used with oatcakes to serve Communion for want of wine and bread at the Battle of Culloden.

The ancient Chinese, Egyptians, Greeks and Romans knew about distillation but the crude spirits they produced were not drunk but used as solvents and unguents. Irish monks may well have had the secret of whisky as a restorative drink in the sixth ,or seventh centuries AD and took it with them when they travelled across to Scotland and into Europe as missionaries. A distillate was a mysterious liquid and was known to preserve dead tissue immersed in it, a property that seemed to associate it with life itself. This 'water of life' was *aqua vitae* in Latin, the *lingua franca* of European scholars at the time, and the name has come down to the modern day.

Left: Boswell and Johnson clearly enjoyed their trip to Scotland. This illustration from Boswell's Journal shows the pair walking "arm-in-arm up the High Street to my home in James Court" in Edinburgh. Opposite page: The evils brought about by the availability of (untaxed) gin in London are portrayed in this etching by William Hogarth, 1751.

Given the Irish connection, however, *aqua vitae* may well be the translation from the Gaelic – *usque baugh* in Irish and *uisge beatha* in Scots – rather than the other way around.

The first written reference to whisky in Scotland is from 1494 when a listing of 'eight bolls of malt to Friar John Cor wherewith to make aquavitae' appears in the Scottish Exchequer Rolls. However whisky had probably already been made for centuries by this time, documentary evidence for it having gone up in smoke in the frequent wars and feuds that typified the era. By the time of good Friar John, whisky was already a developed product, drunk by kings and nobles and, clearly, made in monasteries by monks who were most likely the expert distillers of the day.

There were three qualities of spirit in the days of more primitive equipment, additional distillations endowing more refinement and alcoholic strength. *Simplex* was distilled twice, *composita* three times, and *perfectissima* four times. No whisky is distilled four times today because modern equipment removes the need to do so. Very few producers persevere with three runs and where it is still carried out the main purpose is to preserve the house style of the whisky.

In Highland homes whisky was drunk three times a day partly as a medicinal tonic and partly in the way we take coffee-breaks today. Until recently distilleries carried on a similar routine whereby workers were given three drams daily in the course of their shift as a modest, but universally appreciated, perk. Dr. Johnson enjoyed the whisky served to him during his Highland jaunt with Boswell in 1773 even if the hour in the day surprised him. 'Not long after the dram', he later wrote, 'may be expected the breakfast.'

There was no large-scale production in the Highlands. Whisky making was associated with the home much as baking a cake is today so quantities produced were in proportion to needs. Whisky was also made for sale on a part-time basis by farmers who usually grew barley in addition to other staples like wheat, oats, potatoes, turnips, and so on. They, like everyone else, had access to local peat for fuel and the wonderfully clear water from the burns. Barley could be steeped in any open container or in a pit in the ground; malt dried in a small kiln over a peat fire; the copper worm coil from the tiny battered still would sit in the cold flow of the burn to condense the vapours and the spirit would run into a small cask.

In 1707, Scotland surrendered its political independence in the Act of Union with England and the London Parliament took over the role of the Scottish House in Edinburgh. Imagine, then, the Highlanders' consternation when, with the ink on the document scarcely dry, both malt and whisky became taxable.

In London, primitive gin was made and sold in one house in every four; the death rate, swollen by uncontrolled gin drinking, overtook the birth rate; all restrictions on gin distilling were removed so that English landowners' yearly overproduction of wheat could be absorbed. Yet they decided that it was whisky that had to be taxed!

The Gaels continued to produce their whisky and only very rarely did they pay any duty on it. Ironically, the roadways built throughout the Highlands to enable government soldiers to get into potentially troublesome areas also enabled the smugglers to get their whisky out and down to the bigger markets in the south where

demand outstripped supply. In 1777 there were eight licensed distilleries in Edinburgh and an estimated 400 unlicensed stills. The quality of the licensed product fell right away because distillers had to cut corners massively to pay grotesque duties on their production.

Successive governments could not make up their minds whether they wanted to proscribe whisky distilling or enjoy the revenue it could produce; all through the 18th century and for the first two decades of the 19th, they got it completely wrong. Smugglers' whisky, meanwhile, was of extremely good quality. The illicit distillers had access to the best of raw materials and few overheads. Their whisky was home-made in the best sense and the wholesome product they distilled was the basis for the high standards in the industry.

Whisky was for long drunk as the water-white liquid that ran off the still and there was no reason to think that it might improve in any way if stored. Indeed no doubt it was often even drunk when still warm from the distillation run. Someone will have eventually noticed that whisky from a barrel that had lain unused for a year or so – perhaps an unsold or forgotten puncheon – had lost some of its fire and acquired extra flavour just from its time in the oak container. It was an important discovery whenever it took place, and today Scotch whisky is required by law to age in wood, which means oak.

With the costs of the Napoleonic Wars to meet at the beginning of the 19th century, London had a few more tries at wresting revenue from whisky before the

Duke of Gordon suggested new and fair legislation that would both make distilling viable as a business and yield revenue through reasonable levels of duty. The Excise Act was passed in 1823 and there was an Apache charge of applicants for licences.

Many of the newly respectable distillers were former smugglers and many of the new distilleries were built on the old illicit production sites. Die-hard smugglers burned down the distilleries of a few of the operators who had 'gone legit' and George Smith, later the creator of The Glenlivet whisky, chose to wear a pair of hair-trigger pistols in his belt for some time into the new era. The 1823 legislation was a success, however, and smuggling died out almost completely over the following decade. Many of the distilleries that were built in the 1820s were rebuilt towards the end of the 19th century and this, in turn, is why so many attractive Victorian distilleries have come down to us towards the end of the 20th century.

Scotch has made the best of the opportunities that came its way. It filled the gap created in the 1870s when cognac vanished due to the phylloxera bugs wiping out the Charentes vineyards. Blends were marketed that brought out the best that malt whisky had to offer – i.e. retaining the flavours and aromas, lightening the pungency and giving it consistency. This beat off the threat of distillers in Ireland who refused to blend grain and malt whiskies. In 1909 a Royal Commission, having deliberated for nearly 18 months, decided that grain spirit could indeed be described as whisky and blended Scotch continued to sweep everything before it in becoming the world's favourite drink. Now things have turned full circle with the interest being shown in the individual malt whiskies produced by each distillery. We have the

added advantage today of access to a wide range of bottled single malts instead of just that from the distillery nearest to where we live.

Left: Misty smoke at Glengoyne dries the malt, but in this distillery the smoke is not allowed to infuse the ingredients.
Opposite page, left: Barley is the basic ingredient of whisky. Right: In the mash tun, the dried malt is mashed with hot water to make the wort.

How Whisky is made

Scotch Malt Whisky is made in pot stills from just water, barley and yeast. It is a complicated procedure but basically the traditional method is as follows.

Barley is steeped in water for two or three days, which causes it to start germinating when it is then spread on a maltings floor. Heat is given off and the barley is regularly turned with wooden paddles called shiels to enable even development. Starch in the barley grains turns to sugar over about 12 days, at which time germination is stopped by drying in a kiln. Usually part at least of the drying is by peat-fuelled fires, the smoke from which imparts smoky, peaty aroma and flavour to the malt and the final whisky. This is called peat-reek and can be light or very heavy according to the chosen style. However, one distillery, Glengoyne, closes off the kiln-smoke from the malt so that no smokiness goes into the whisky.

The dried malt is ground into grist and mashed (mixed) together with hot water to make a sugar-rich liquid called wort. It is drawn off and the solids left behind are collected for use as cattle feed. (Quite a few distillery herds have won Supreme Championships at Smithfield over the years.) The wort has yeast added to it, which then ferments over two days into a weak ale called wash.

Most pot-still whisky is distilled twice so stills tend to be grouped in pairs comprising a wash still and a spirit still. There are a few distilleries where a third still is used either to allow more complicated production methods (e.g. Springbank) or for triple distillation (e.g. Auchentoshan). With double-distillation, the wash is loaded into the wash still which is heated (sometimes with a naked coal or gas flame, usually these days with internal steam pipes) to slow boiling. Alcohol vapours boil off, pass over the still's swan-neck and condense (rarely now in a 'worm' immersed in cold water, usually in a modern condenser) to a liquid, called low wines. The low wines are then loaded into the spirit still and distilled a second time.

As the distillate begins to run off, the early part is unwholesome and steered to a side tank by the stillman watching the liquid pass through the spirit safe. At the right moment, he diverts the flow and collects the next part of the run in the main container which is called the spirit receiver.

The stillman must continue to watch because while the liquid runs off the still, its alcoholic strength gradually drops. When a fixed strength is reached the flow is once again turned away to the side tank until it peters out, almost as water. The 'middle cut' – the 'heart' of the run that was collected in the spirit receiver – is the clean, wholesome distillate which goes on to become whisky. Nothing is wasted. The foreshots and feints that were collected separately are added to the next batch of low wines and distilled with them.

Scotch Grain Whisky is made in continuous stills from assorted unmalted cereals and a proportion of malted barley. The unmalted grains are cooked so that the starch cells burst open. When they are mixed with the malted barley to make a mash, the starch turns to sugar and a wort is created as with malt whisky production.

The fermented wash is fed in a constant flow to a patent still which completes both the evaporation and condensation processes within its analyser and rectifier columns. As long as wash is fed in, spirit comes out at the other end. The grain spirit is produced at much higher strength, making it smooth in texture but faint in both flavour and aroma.

Both malt and grain whisky must age in oak casks for a legal minimum of three years, but in fact most ages for much longer. The majority of single malts mature for between eight and 16 years, and 12 years is widely used as the bottling age for both malts and good *de luxe* blends. If an age is declared on a label it refers to the youngest whisky blended or vatted in the bottle.

During ageing, whisky loses its youthful fieriness and takes on flavours and aromas from the cask. Vanilla and a pleasant oakiness are two such, and, if the cask has previously held sherry, sweetness, toffee and sherry flavours may also come through. With a range of characteristics on call, the best whiskies achieve a balance of mellowness, complexity and completeness that is most attractive.

Blended Scotch assembles the best degrees of whisky's richness, flavour, aroma,

texture, mellowness and strength without the more daunting extremes of pungency, concentration, high strength, ultra-smokiness or blandness. Blended Scotch has nothing in common with, say, blended wine or blended

Above: The swan-necks at the top of the stills carry off the alcohol vapours. These stills are at Teaninich. Left: The stillman at Aberlour distillery checks the strength of the spirit as it passes through the spirit safe.

whiskey from other countries where something acceptable is made out of constituents that are unbalanced or flawed. Most of the whiskies used in blended Scotch are available as self whiskies in their own right. Good blends have from 45% to 60% malt content and the skills needed to assemble perhaps 45 different whiskies to make a single consistent blend are considerable.

Styles of Whisky

Scotch whisky divides into three main styles: malt, grain and a blend of these two.

• **Malt Whisky** has specific, sometimes very pronounced, flavours and aromas which come from the malted barley, the amount of peat used in drying it and, once ageing is completed, the type of wood in which it matures. The range of character goes from deep, pungent, smoky and earthy to light, subtle, gentle and sweet. A single malt is the whisky produced by an individual distillery. A vatted malt is a blend of malts from two or more individual distilleries.

• **Grain Whisky** is easier, and hence cheaper, to produce and its quieter personality makes it often, but not always, less interesting as a self whisky. Grain spirit matures rapidly so tends to need less ageing than malts. Most grain whisky is used in blending to soften and lighten the final product but there are two distilleries which put stated-age single grains in bottle, one of these launched quite recently.

• **Blended Whisky** is a blend of both malt and grain whiskies. Each brand of blended whisky is made to a specific, secret recipe and well-known brands like Famous Grouse and Bell's have many different single distillates in their make-up.

Types of Still

• **A Pot Still** is simply a large kettle, which is filled to a certain capacity with wash so it can be boiled off. The alcoholic vapours rise to the top of the swan-neck, pass over and run through cold pipes which condense them back to liquid. A first distillation creates a liquid of about 8 per cent alcohol by volume. Most pot-still production is by double-distillation and after the second distilling run the spirit reaches about 70 per cent alcohol by volume.

• **A Continuous Still** is a more complex machine, which ingeniously combines the boiling and condensation processes in tall rectification towers so that spirit is produced in a continuous flow. Distillate from a continuous still is usually high in strength and smooth in texture; a drawback, however, is that most of the flavouring elements are lost. Alternative names for these stills are 'patent' or Coffey, the latter after the Irish Exciseman who developed the original idea; Stein, the Scottish inventor of the continuous process, receives scant credit today for his achievement.

Different Kinds of Barrel

The oak barrels in which Scotch ages mostly come from Spain and the USA. The Spanish casks are brought over from Jerez and have previously been used to ferment and/or store sherry, usually oloroso. This imparts a rich, sweet finish to the whisky, accounting for as much, some say, as 50 per cent of the final flavour and texture. The traditions of using Spanish sherrywood go back a long way to the days when sherry was imported in barrels and bottled here. The sherry overlay on the whisky became

such an accepted part of the style that the interiors of non-sherry barrels were often coated with cooked wine concentrates called paxarete before being filled with new spirit. This is no longer done.

Those casks brought from the USA have previously held bourbon. Since by American law each can only be used once, they become redundant as soon as they are emptied for the whiskey to be bottled. Scotch companies that prefer not to use sherry casks mature spirit in ex-bourbon wood, because subtler natural flavours in their whiskies can show through more readily.

Very few distillers use all-sherry or all-bourbon wood, most deciding on a (secret) combination of the two. Further subtleties may be achieved by using casks that have been filled with Scotch once, twice or three times before. With each filling, the influence that a cask can have on the whisky is diminished.

Regional Classification of Whisky Styles

If malt whisky were French it would, like wine and cognac, be legally divided into a dozen or so *appellations contrôlées* based on features such as analysis of water supply, specified barley types, and peat content in parts per million. The classification that actually exists is a conventional four-part division which has only recently become properly useful by the adoption of certain sub-divisions.

Highland is the largest and most diverse category comprising the mainland and islands (except Islay) north of a line drawn diagonally between the Firth of Clyde and the Firth of Tay. Although there are earthy, full-throated exceptions – especially near the coasts – the whiskies are mainly light/medium-weight and fragrant.

Two important sub-divisions are Speyside and Island. Speyside is the area around the River Spey and tributaries in the north-east. Gentle, green, fertile countryside that yields richly aromatic and flavoured malts within a light-to-medium and well-balanced framework. Very elegant with good complexity.

Island includes the inner islands off the west (Jura, Mull and Skye) and north (Orkney) coasts of Scotland, where style includes Highland elegance but stretches to full-bodied smoky peatiness, concentration, spiciness and a zest of salty ozone.

An addition to this group is pending with the scheduled completion of a new distillery on the island of Arran. It is to be the island's first for 150 years.

• **Lowland** malts are from the mainland to the south of that Highland Line mentioned above. They are soft and understated, often sweet, smooth and whispery malts with faint delivery in peatiness compared to any of the other categories.

• **Islay** is a category in its own right due to the pungent, concentrated and peaty earthiness of the traditional style of whisky produced there. Tasters speak of seashore and even medicinal dimensions to the richness of the prevailing character yet the whiskies have their own remarkable structure and balance. Despite its particularity, traditional Islay whisky is becoming very popular outside Scotland, although some distillers are choosing to lighten the style in the brands they produce.

• **Campbeltown** is such a diminished category now that it is shared by only two distilleries producing three whiskies; it used to be the second-largest grouping after Highland. The malts are rich and quite full-bodied with a distinct saltiness and medium-impact peat. When there were more distilleries it was regarded as a halfway house between mainland and Islay styles.

Peat

Looking across a peat bog on to mountains is to take a mental snapshot of the landscape as it was in prehistoric times. All that is likely to have changed in the view before you is the thickness of the carpet – 10 metres of depth takes about 8000 years to form. It is formed by the build-up of successive layers of seasonal fen vegetation which cannot decompose due to waterlogging and lack of oxygen. Peat occurs uniformly across the Scottish landcape so it is no surprise that it has long been the traditional household fuel. Its role in the Gaels' whisky making was fortuitous since it was burned simply to dry the malted barley – what else were they going to use?

Early experimentation in generating electricity from a peat-burning turbine was carried out in 1959 at Altnabreac Bog in Caithness (about 30 miles west of Pulteney distillery). Peat is now used to fire power stations and, although it has about two-thirds of the calorific value of coal, the cost per unit of electricity generated is less than that of coal. As well as its use in whisky making, peat is used in the fish-curing industry in Scotland.

Opposite: The spirit is left to mature in wooden barrels in the distillery warehouses.
Left: Cutting peat on the moor near Highland Park.

Trail 1 North Highlands
From Inverness to Kirkwall

Introduction

This trail follows the string of distilleries up the stretch of Scotland's east coast that lies to the north of Inverness, the capital of the Highlands. All the distilleries are in the Highland category of malts, although some like to describe Orkney's two malts as Island products.

Inverness itself no longer has an active distillery. Two distilleries that were, until very recently, in production were Glen Albyn and Glen Mhor, both of which are alternative Gaelic names for the Great Glen, through whose length the Caledonian Canal passes. Both shared the same water source, Loch Ness, and production of both was stopped in the 1980s. It is still possible to find bottles of Glen Albyn and Glen Mhor from independents.

Above: Loch Ness, to the south of Inverness, provides a scenic start to the first whisky trail. In the past, the Loch provided water for distilleries in the area.

Glen Ord Distillery

Location: Muir of Ord, Ross-shire • Roads: By the A832
Season: **All year • *Hours:* 9.30pm – 4.15pm, Mon – Fri**
July – August Sat. 9.30 – 4.15; Sun 12.30 – 4.15
November – February : Restricted hours
Group bookings by appointment
Reception centre, shop and exhibition • *Tel:* 01463-871334

*T*he Ord, 15 miles north of Inverness, the Highland capital, is a great flat expanse of land between the shore and the hills. Many a clan battle took place here but most of the time it was the site of market trysts to which droves of cattle, horses and sheep came from all directions.

This is Mackenzie country and clan castles – serene Eilean Donan, Kintail and Brahan – lie mainly to the west. In the 18th century, Brahan, near Ord, was the home of the remarkable Coineach Odhar, widely known as the Scottish Nostradamus. Known as the Brahan Seer, he forecast important future events in minute detail – most of them properly documented – and for his trouble was boiled in oil on a headland near Ord for 'dabbling in witchcraft'.

The distillery was lit by paraffin lamps until it came on to the national electricity grid after World War II but water power was used for some operations right up to the early 1960s.

In 1598, Thomas Mackenzie bought the Ord area, built Ord House and began farming. Both his alehouse and the House were fed by the Allt Fionnaidh burn with pristine water, and it was the same supply tapped by a kinsman, Alexander Mackenzie, in 1838 when he built his distillery. Things went well enough for successive owners over the years although there were difficult times which saw the business placed under sequestration orders.

There were nine other licensed stills in the area so the competition for business was stiff. All of the local barley crop was used for distillation – the fastest way to turn raw materials into cash. Whisky was the only manufactured product in the area. One proprietor in the 1870s went bankrupt and died. His pragmatic widow saw to it that this would not happen again by marrying a bank agent, from Beauly, whom she put in charge of the business.

Glen Ord whisky was sold far afield, going out to Singapore, South Africa and other British colonies. The distillery became part of DCL after it failed in 1923.

The peat is cut from local moss in spring, taken to the distillery in autumn and dried before use. In the past it could be left for up to four years in order to get the best results. Today, Glen Ord's drum maltings operation supplies malted barley to many other distilleries in the north and west of Scotland, so much more peat than Glen Ord distillery could use is brought in and stacked in readiness. Entire sheds lie overbrimming with it at Glen Ord. Malting today is a surprisingly noisy business, as the ventilated kiln fires roar like jet engines.

Glen Ord is one of a number of distilleries that have a single glass wall to the stillhouse, enabling the giant copper stills to be seen from outside. The pagoda heads are still in place.

The floor maltings were used until 1961 when they were converted to a Saladin Box operation. This was a system that replaced the maltman turning malt by hand with mechanical turners that ran constantly up and down a malting trough. This is no longer in operation but the long, low-sided concrete box is still in position and may be seen during the distillery tour.

Glen Ord was the site of an eight-year experimentation programme to compare coal, oil and steam as means of heating the stills. From 1958 onwards, batches of spirit were produced by each fuel and monitored to see if they varied; as a result, when the distillery's two previously coal-fired stills were increased to six in 1966, all of them were fitted with steam-heated coils.

One of the local smuggling stories concerns Excisemen taking a confiscated

Above: At Glen Ord Distillery, steam-heated coils have replaced coal-fired stills, but the oak casks give the spirit a smoky sweetness.

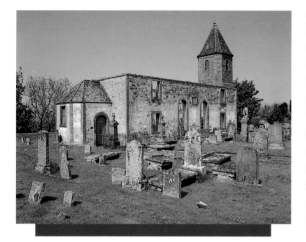

cask of whisky upstairs to their bedroom in an inn to safeguard the evidence overnight. By drilling up through the ceiling below and the bottom of the cask, the smugglers' cronies 'liberated' the whisky into a succession of jugs and removed the evidence at the same time. The inn in question is said to be the Bogroy Hotel at nearby Beauly; ask at the bar and they'll show you the hole!

Above: A ruined Gaelic chapel overlooks the well-preserved, quiet township of Cromarty.

The Whisky

A succession of names has been used for the single malt sold in bottle. In the 1880s some Ord whisky was sold in bottle as Glen Oran. Then it was simply Ord, next came the slightly kitsch Glenordie, and now it has recently been relaunched as Glen Ord. It is lightly peated but shows good round flavour with some smoky sweetness at the finish. 'Perilously drinkable,' someone once said.

It is 12 years old and 40% vol. Special vintage one-offs and different ages by independent bottlers are rare. It is used in the make-up of Dewar's blended Scotch.

Of interest nearby

• **Cromarty** on the Black Isle to the east is the Highlands' best-preserved 18th century town, 'the jewel in the crown of Scottish vernacular architecture.' Both Georgian grandeur and pawky crow-stepped gables intermingle around the town. One of the buildings is the **Court House** of 1773 which is now a 'live' museum. Sit in on a trial with life-size animated figures. Cromarty also has a 19th-century ice-house and its lighthouse was built by Robert Louis Stevenson's uncle.
• **Dolphin Ecosse** boat trips take in World War I gun emplacements, shipwrecks and bottlenose dolphins.
• Slightly weird is the **Clootie Well** at Munlochy, where strips of cloth (clootie) festoon trees that overhang the running water of the spring. To tie a piece of cloth on a branch is to bring good luck, they say, and the well is surprising evidence that so many people take the trouble to do so.
• The **Highland Museum of Childhood** at Strathpeffer has themed events and a dressing-up box for children.

1

Dalmore Distillery

Location: **Alness, Ross-shire IV17 0UT**
Roads: **Off A9 north of Inverness**
Seasons: **Mid-Aug. to early-June, except mid-Dec. to mid-Jan.**
Hours: **All visits by appointment only. Group bookings, max 10**
No reception centre or shop • *Tel:* 01349-882362

*A*lexander Matheson was a partner in the dynastic Hong Kong trading firm, Jardine Matheson & Co. In the early days these merchants dealt in everything from tea to opium, the latter commodity the reason that the British took root there in the first place. In 1839, the very year that the First Opium War broke out between China and Britain, Matheson bought Ardross farm, on the shore of the Cromarty Firth near the village of Alness, and set about improving it; one of the facilities he added was a still.

Much of the whisky produced in Scotland in the 18th century came from Easter Ross and Dalmore was one of the new distilleries built in the area in the wake of the 1823 Act, which made distilling both viable and legal. The distillery sits in a beautiful spot on the shore of the Cromarty Firth north of Inverness.

During the early years the distillery was leased to the Sutherland family, with the

1

lease then passing to Robert Pattison in the mid 1860's. The tenancy then passed to the Mackenzie family in 1867, who eventually took ownership in 1891. Andrew Mackenzie was the moving force of the Mackenzie brothers and impudently included Speyside in their sales patch for Dalmore whisky. He was also something of a good cricketer, playing for a local team and usually able to put a good score on the board.

Ownership remained with the Mackenzies until 1960 when it was bought by the Glasgow based Whyte & Mackay Group.

Peat and barley were locally grown and coal to fire Dalmore's stills came in to Alness station from the Fife colleries via the newly opened railway line. A single railway line used to connect the distillery with the main line at Alness station, which in the old days, was a rallying point for the Highlanders from the north against the Southerners.

This railway line enabled barley and coal etc. to be delivered direct into the premises. The pier at Belleport on the Cromarty Firth forms part of the distillery property and also allowed shipments of barley, coals, coke and other stores to be unloaded at its door from the steamers.

During World War 1, £1 million worth of maturing whisky was removed to three other distilleries in the area and Dalmore's warehouses were requisitioned by the Admiralty as a mine-making factory, It was 1920 before the distillery was handed

back and the whisky returned, with not a single cask missing.

Dalmore's make figures in all the parent company's blended brands and the Mackenzie connection is remembered on the Dalmore labels with the stag's head emblem, the badge of the Mackenzie clan.

In 1956 a Saladin box system of malting was installed and operated until 1981, when malting production ceased.

The distillery acquired sole rights to draw its water from the River Alness which flows from the beautiful Loch of Kildermorie, close to Ben Wyvis. Production began with a single pair pair of stills and a second pair was added in a separate stillhouse in 1874. The upper part of those 1874 stills has survived and is still in use today. It is unusual in outline, having parallel sides instead of the customary tapering swan-neck. Dalmores' stills are cooled by running water over the outside of the stillnecks in a way that is similar to the temperature control on fermentation vats in wine making. There are now four pairs of stills, the latter four units dating from 1966.

Dalmore covers 25 acres, much of that space taken up with the warehouses where the spirit matures. There are about 100,000 casks on site. The oldest whisky still mellowing there in wood is a 1939 distillation.

The Whisky

In Andrew Mackenzie's day, there were two qualities. The better one was aged in sherrywood, the standard in new casks called distillery wood. The whisky was aged for up to six years and often the two styles were vatted together, the proportions depending on the customer's taste. Today, large batches of casks with 12- to 15-year-old Dalmore are vatted (blended) and then kept in sherrywood until bottled.

The whisky is quite full in flavour but shows elegance of finish. A mite smoky, naturally dryish but showing sweet-edged because of the sherry background. Twelve-year-old and 40/43% vol.; the same age from different wood may be had from one of the independents.

Teaninich Distillery

Location: **Alness, Ross-shire**
Closed to visitors

*T*eaninich was founded prior to the watershed 1823 Act in 1817, but the distillery today is a modern plant of box-shaped buildings and tall chimneys.

It has 12 stills and distils high volumes of spirit principally for blending. Like Dalmore, Teaninich began as an estate distillery but the laird himself, Captain Hugh Munro, ran it as part of the whole. It was only in 1852 that the operation was first leased out to a licensee, Robert Pattison. The last vestiges of the old distillery disappeared under the 1974 rebuilding programme.

Teaninich was the first distillery north of Inverness to install electric light and one of the first to have an internal telephone system. It is, in a sense, two distilleries since there are two distinct sides, each operating as a complete unit, but all spirit is merged to create a single product.

The Whisky

Teaninich is one of the whiskies used in the production of the famous liqueur, Drambuie (*see page 148*), and occasionally one-off private bottlings take place. Some 1971, 1975, 1982 and 27-year-old at 40% vol. were recently traceable. It is a soft, smoky and floral spirit, probably used in blending for texture and finish.

Of interest nearby

• **Mutch Woodturning Workshop** offers tuition in a range of wood-working crafts.

Invergordon Grain + Ben Wyvis Distillery

Location: **Invergordon, Ross-shire**
Closed to visitors

Some dramatic events have taken place at Invergordon, mainly to do with its status as a naval base. In 1915 ammunition carried in a cruiser blew up and 400 men died; in 1931 the Invergordon Mutiny took place; and it has become the repair yard to the great floating rigs of North Sea oil.

It is also remembered for the performance just before World War II of a BBC radio commentator in the days when broadcasting meant going live. Expected to give a rousing commentary to the listening nation on the night-time splendour of the fleet assembled to send Hitler packing, all he could produce was the repeating expression that 'the fleetsh all lit up, all lit up, itsh ... itsh ... lovely and ... all lit up.'

He could not have been drinking Invergordon whisky, however, because this complex, the only grain distillery in the Highlands, did not begin producing until 1961. It was a conscious effort to bring work to the northern Highlands and the plant is now the largest of its kind in Europe.

Grain spirit for blending and neutral alcohol are produced on a unique still, designed in-house as a development of the Coffey still. The grain whisky is used for the company's blending, sold to the industry and traded for malt whiskies. Ben Wyvis is a malt whisky distillery with a single pair of stills on the same site, but has been silent since 1977. It is an extremely rare spirit.

The Whisky

Recently, Invergordon began bottling a single grain whisky – one of only two in the whole of Scotland – to serve modern consumer interest in unblended Scotch from individual distilleries. It is 10 years old; silky and light in texture, gently wooded and fragrant, with a pleasant bite from 43% vol. alcohol.

Glenmorangie Distillery

Location: **Tain, Ross-shire IV19 1PZ**
Roads: **A9, signposted just north of Tain** • *Seasons:* **All year**
Hours: **Tours 10.30am and 2.30pm, Tues, Wed & Thurs** •
All visits by appointment • **Group bookings, max 10**
No reception centre or shop • *Tel:* **01862-892043** *Fax:* **01862-393862**

Glenmorangie is the best-selling malt whisky in Scotland and the distillery that makes it sits at the bottom of a slope on the shore of the Dornoch Firth. The setting is very much a little 'glen of tranquillity', as the translation from the Gaelic describes it. Glenmorangie is close to the Royal Burgh of Tain, one of Scotland's oldest towns and long a place of pilgrimage due to its being the birthplace of St Duthus around the year 1000 AD.

Assorted buildings climb the slope above the warehouses at the water's edge and in summer stone-built distillery cottages are smothered in flowers. A waterwheel that used to supply all the power is still in place. The staff comprises the 'Sixteen Men of Tain' who make the whisky and they are featured in the company's advertising; all are local celebrities. A recently retired manager had worked at the distillery for 40 years and his father for 70 years before him.

Documentation about distilling at the old Morangie farmhouse goes back at least 250 years to the 1730s, but the licensed activity began in 1843 with the conversion of a brewery by William Mathieson. By the 1880s the distillery was very run down and new owners completely rebuilt it. The buildings today date from that time

1

although a further internal rebuilding took place in 1979, including the installation of two more stills.

The water at Glenmorangie is hard and 100 years old by the time it bubbles up in the Tarlogie Springs, which can be visited in the adjacent woodland. Before modern filtration systems were installed, limescale had to be laboriously chipped away from the inside of the boilers during the summer months, when the distillery was closed. The company have safeguarded future water supply by buying the springs and surrounding land.

Glenmorangie is effectively produced entirely for bottling as a single malt, but some is used for blending in certain of the company's own brands. The old-style warehouses have earthen floors, which absorb moisture in wet weather and humidify the air around the casks during the hot summer weather.

Glenmorangie was the first distillery in Scotland to use steam to heat the stills instead of the customary coal fires, which often caused off-flavours through scorching. Eight stills (four pairs) are in place now, including two each from the years 1977, 1980 and 1990. Pot stills have a lifespan of about 15 years and when replaced exact copies must be supplied to avoid the risk of altering the nature of the spirit. Glenmorangie's are the tallest in Scotland (almost 17 feet), which is an important factor in creating the whisky's elegant house style. Also contributory to this is the 'boil pot' each of them has – a bulge below the neck of the still which ensures that only the lightest, finest alcohols pass over in distillation.

In an on-going comparative study, a cask of bourbon whiskey from the Maker's Mark distillery in Kentucky, USA, is maturing at Glenmorangie to see how the spirit ages in the cooler, damper atmosphere. An equivalent cask of Glenmorangie is undergoing maturation in the hothouse warehouse at Maker's Mark.

Glenmorangie has recently introduced a Wood Finishes range. The whisky is matured in its traditional barrels but then finished for up to two years in Port wood, Maderia wood or Sherry wood.

The Whisky

Glenmorangie uses only American ex-Bourbon oak for maturation of its whisky, all barrels being discarded after the third refill stage. This is one of the few Scotch malts that uses no sherrywood whatsoever in the maturation of its main style. It is deliberate due to the fact that Glenmorangie whisky, although complex, is very subtle. A French parfumier detected 26 distinct aromas in the spirit, enhancing elements that Glenmorangie prefer to cherish and foster rather than mask with sherry-aging. This does not prevent the distillery finishing off certain older special edition bottlings with some months in sherry casks since more mature spirit is a little more assertive. The standard whisky is 10 years old at 40% vol. It is delicate, fruity

and flowery with some sweetness and bite. The Glenmorangie Natural cask strength is the same age but about 59% vol.-it tends to have a fuller, nuttier, spicier flavour. The 18-year-old at 43% vol. is rounder in texture with vanilla, honey and caramel from time spent in small oak casks.

Above: A cooper at Glenmorangie fits a bung, using sackcloth to give a perfect fit. Above right: All barrels in the warehouse are re-used; most come from the American bourbon trade.

Of interest nearby

• The **Poor House** at Tain dates from the 1840s. Under the Poor Law Act, parishes had to provide for the needy but often the places were so austere that paupers turned down the offer of admission tickets. Potatoes, oatmeal and vegetables - never meat-made up the staple diet; nowadays all these foods have come to be highly regarded by nutritionists.

• **Cheesemakers** at Blairliath in Tain welcome visitors. There are free tastings and conducted tours.

Balblair Distillery

Location: **Edderton, Tain, Ross-shire IV19 1LB**
Seasons: **September - June**
Hours: **10am - 12 noon, 2pm - 4pm, Mon - Thur**
All visits by appointment • Group bookings, max 8
No reception centre • *Tel:* **01862-821273**

This is Ross-shire, the old territory of the Clan Ross, so it is appropriate that a well-known local whisky-making family of the same name had much to do with running the two distilleries called Balblair. Today it is claimed to be the second-oldest distillery in Scotland. Edderton lies just up the A9 from Glenmorangie and has a similarly beautiful setting overlooking the shore of the Dornoch Firth. On the opposite shore lie Spinningdale, where Mackintosh produced coats from his new waterproof material, and Dornoch, where the 'last witch in Scotland' was burned in 1722. The second Balblair construction was a continuation of the business and, with its stone-built, Victorian neatness, is one of the prettiest little distilleries in Scotland.

Distilling at Balblair enters the record in 1749 but 1790 is given as the founding of the distillery. Even this is an early date since few of today's distilling names were in existence before the turn of the 19th century. In the 1860s, Andrew Ross's son, John, went down to Alness to work the Teaninich distillery and Balblair was rebuilt about half a mile away from the original site. The new buildings were on higher ground so that use could be made of gravity in working the distillery, but also to be closer to the railway line. The old buildings down below became warehouses.

The distillery was closed from 1915 to 1947 when it was bought by a Keith solicitor called Cumming who also owned Pulteney distillery up at Wick. Balblair was sold to Inver House in 1996 having been owned by Hiram Walker

The water used in production comes down from lochs high in the hills nearby. Balblair's owners supply their own barley seeds to farmers in Fife so that they can have maximum control over pre-production factors. Edderton is surrounded by peat

1

Left: Spinningdale, the home of the Mackintosh, lies across the Dornoch Firth from the Balblair Distillery.

that goes light and crumbly when seasoned, helping to impart finesse and subtlety to the final whisky. Appropriately, the village is known as 'the parish of peats'.

This is a fine example of a small, country distillery and the buildings are pretty well as they were at the end of the 19th century; the long closure from 1915 helped things remain intact. On-site malting ended in the mid-1970s but the old steeps and part of the building are still in place. One of the washbacks was brought from Ardbeg distillery on Islay and one of the three stills is finished with rivets, which is the old-fashioned method of sealing seams on stills.

The Whisky

Balblair is bottled at five and ten years old with 40% vol. It is typically light with medium peat presence; spice and a consistent bite show through at all ages. Some 1959, 1964 and 26-year-old have recently been offered by the independents, plus another 10-year-old from different wood from that used at the distillery. Balblair is used in Ballantine's Scotch blends.

Of interest nearby

• **Croick Church** at Ardgay became the refuge for tenants evicted from their holdings by landowners during the Highland Clearances in 1845 to make way for sheep. Ask to see the names the refugees scratched on the east window at the time.
• **Carbisdale Castle**, which looms imposingly above the forest to the north-west, is probably the grandest youth hostel in Europe.
• The **Falls of Shin** near Lairg give a grandstand view (at the right times of the year) of salmon leaping and often actually swimming up the tumbling, white-water cascade.

Clynelish Distillery

Location: **Brora, Sutherland KW9 6LR** • *Roads:* **Off the A9 at Brora**
Seasons: **March–Oct, 9.30am - 4.00pm, Mon – Fri**
Group bookings by appointment • Reception centre and shop
Tel: **01408-621444/ 621033** • *Fax:* **01408-621131**

*T*he River Brora has a reputation for fine salmon and the town of the same name has an attractive little harbour. Brora is a small resort now but in 1529 they opened a coalmine (the only one in the Highlands) and in the 17th century a saltworks was set up. The brickworks got going in 1818, just a year before the distillery. Successive Earls of Sutherland, the local lairds in their castle at Golspie, saw to it that Brora was always a working town. Then they changed tack and evicted just about everyone from the entire county and put in sheep instead – the infamous Highland Clearances. Such was the extent of their landownership, that the Sutherlands were able to empty 500,000 acres of 15,000 people; in a single night in 1819, the year that the distillery was built, 250 crofts were burned.

Just as there were two locations in the story of Balblair at Edderton, Clynelish is the latterday form of a separate distillery set up in 1819 by the Marquis of Stafford (later Duke of Sutherland). Hence, most of the history belongs to the original distillery, which was renamed Brora (*see page 34*), when the new structure built alongside took over the Clynelish name.

The new Clynelish went into production in 1967. It is attractive in the modern way, but anonymous. Land from Clynelish Farm was acquired and water supplies were augmented from the Clynemilton Burn.

The new Clynelish is three times the size of the original and has three pairs of stills. It very much continues the tradition of the original Clynelish

1

The Whisky

Distilleries do not need to be old to produce good whisky and with modern technology nothing need be left to chance. Clynelish is one of the most powerful Highland malts with a rich, salty earthiness more readily associated with Island styles. This is often attributed to the proximity of the sea, but what about the shoreline malts – Glenmorangie, Oban and others – which show no marine characteristics? This is all part of the mystery of malt whisky.

Available at 14 years and 43% vol. as well as cask-strength 1972 vintage, 12- and 20-year-old from independents, and exported as a 22 year old Rare Malt at 58.6% alc.

Of interest nearby

• **Dunrobin Castle** is the seat of the Dukes of Sutherland, set on a raised rock pedestal. A 13th-century keep lies within the 19th-century, French-inspired outer; the rooms are sumptuously decorated and full of Louis XV furniture. The gardens are based on those at Versailles.

• **Carn Liath Broch** lies north of Dunrobin, a well-preserved example of the round towers, usually with stairways in hollow walls, that are among the few tangible legacies of the Picts.

Above: Set in delightful gardens on a rocky outcrop, the castle at Dunrobin has a Disneyesque appeal.

1

Brora Distillery

Location: **Brora, Sutherland** • *Roads:* **Off the A9**

Brora distillery closed in 1983 and ceded its original name – Clynelish – to the new distillery built just across the road from it. Brora, viewed from the outside with its hump-backed hill rising behind, is a fine example of the classic, close-knit little

Victorian distillery – steeply sloping warehouse roofs, an imperious pagoda head rising high above everything but the chimney-stack and a fort-like cluster of stone buildings round a courtyard.

The distillery was founded in 1819 by the Marquis of Stafford who had married into the Sutherland family. His idea was at least partly to take control of local whisky-supply away from the smugglers. There were several licensees up to 1834 when Andrew Ross took over for a dozen years. In 1896, Glasgow blenders, Ainslie's, bought the distillery and rebuilt it to the form it has today, and the distillery eventually passed to DCL. There is one pair of stills and the floor maltings and kiln are still in place.

Above: If you take a torch, you can crawl into the corbelled interior of the Grey Cairns of Camster.

The Whisky

It is still possible to find Brora malt. When Clynelish and Brora were both in production, the latter initially produced spirit from very highly peated barley to produce an Islay type of whisky for blending; it then went over to using the same milder reek as Clynelish. There was no in-house bottling of Brora as a single malt, but casks were acquired by independents. Currently available is 1972, from one of the High Street specialists, which is in the concentrated style. It is quite splendidly earthy, spicy and resonant à la Islay, but the texture and finish are unexpectedly elegant and clean. Last distillations took place in 1983 so, theoretically, there could be surprise packages around for some time yet.

Of interest nearby

• There was a **Goldrush** in the 1860s in the Strath of Kildonan. **Baile an Or** ('Valley of Gold') and **Suisgill** were the main lodes and gold is still found today; you can get a permit to pan from the Information centre at Helmsdale.
• Did the Scots beat Columbus to the discovery of America? The **Clan Gunn Heritage Centre** at Latheron has the evidence, they say.
• **Laidhay Croft Museum** at Dunbeath is a rush-thatched Caithness longhouse with the stable, byre and living quarters under a single roof.
• The **Grey Cairns of Camster** are chambered tombs from 4000 BC built of Caithness flagstone.

Pulteney Distillery

Location: **Wick, Caithness KW1 5BA**
Roads: **Huddart Street in Pulteneytown suburb**
Please telephone for information about visits • *Tel:* 01955-602371

*W*ick lies in the far north-eastern corner of Scotland, less than 20 miles from John O'Groats where the land runs out. Wick was a Royal Burgh in the 16th century but it was the 19th-century herring industry based there that brought both notoriety and prosperity. So many fishing craft crammed the bay – often a thousand at a time – that the masts looked like defoliated woodland and people could walk across the great harbour by passing from one boat to the next. So wild was the town that the authorities had to declare prohibition for a time; a dry town with a distillery in full production!

Much of the town is built in the distinctive local Caithness flagstone, the structure of which may be seen on the coast road as the littoral rises to run along the clifftop. Dramatically sited castle ruins are scattered about, Wick, Sinclair and Girnigoe being among the best known. Pultneytown on the southern side of the harbour was built by Thomas Telford as a planned fishing village and the streets were named after his own friends. It was later improved by the engineer Thomas Stevenson, and his famous son, Robert Louis, author of *Treasure Island*, lived with him in the town while the work was carried out.

Like Oban and only one or two other distilleries, Pulteney is in a town setting. It is the northernmost distillery on the mainland (two more, remember, on Orkney)

Right: The most northerly town of mainland Scotland, John O'Groats is less than 20 miles north of the Pultney Distillery. Famous for its position, John O'Groats has a small fishing industry. However, you will have to travel on to Thurso to get a ferry to Orkney.

and was established in 1826 by James Henderson, already a seasoned distiller with 30 years' (probably illicit) experience further inland. Pulteney remained in the family's hands for almost a century and bottles of their Henderson brand of whisky are displayed at the distillery. A decade after it was sold Pulteney closed and did not reopen for 21 years when it was bought by R. Cumming, the Banff lawyer who had also bought Balblair (*qv*). He in turn sold on to Hiram Walker, who rebuilt the distillery in 1959. It was sold to Inver House in 1995.

The water used for cooling the distillation is run from Loch Hempriggs in a lade designed by Thomas Telford. Although Victorian in date, much of the distinctive structural appearance of a distillery of its time has disappeared. The maltings were taken out of use in 1959. Two stills are in place now but at the turn of the century there were three. The two very small spirit stills in use then were subsequently removed and a single large unit installed to take their place. Both of the present stills are distinctively, rather oddly shaped, but since they produce the Pulteney signature in the spirit, the dimensions will never be changed; replacements will always be exact copies. Mostly bourbon casks are used to mature Pulteney spirit and the warehouses on site can accommodate about 30,000 of them.

The Whisky

Pulteney is yet another coastal whisky, with an earthy, pungent character, although it shares the lightness and smoky cleanness of Clynelish and Brora rather than the simmering concentration of Skye and Islay. Indeed it is sometimes described as the 'Manzanilla of the North', referring to the tangy, salty style created when certain sherries are matured on the Mediterranean coast near Jerez in southern Spain.

Pulteney is bottled at a younger age than most malts - eight years at 40% vol. –
due to its reputation for rapid maturation. Further choice is available from the
independents – 12-, 15- and 22-year-old, as well as 1961 vintage, being recently on
offer and sometimes described as Old Pulteney. The distillery's whisky is one of the
malts used in the make-up of Ballantine's blended brands.

*Above: High on a headland, the spectacular castles of Sinclair and Girnigoe are just a few
miles from the centre of Wick.*

Of interest nearby

• **Wick Heritage Centre** has a kippering kiln, a cooperage and a blacksmith's shop
in its absorbing evocation of the town's rich past. There is also a remarkable
photographic collection, with over 100,000 glass negatives of Victorian Wick.

• **Caithness Glass** welcomes visitors to watch hand-blown glass production in its
workshops near the airport.

• Castles pepper the country around Wick, many of them wonderfully atmospheric
ruins in spectacular clifftop settings like **Sinclair** and **Girnigoe**. Others have
become comfortable hotels like **Ackergill Tower** where television personality
Philip Schofield had his wedding reception.

Highland Park Distillery

Location: **Kirkwall, Orkney KW15 1SU** • *Roads:* **Holm Road**
Seasons: **April – October, 10am – 5pm Mon – Fri;**
also July – August, Sat/ Sun 12.00 – 5.00pm;
November – March, tours only at 2.00 and 3.30pm, Mon – Fri
Tours every 1/2 hour; last tour at 4.00pm
Group bookings by appointment
Reception centre, audio–visual presentation and shop
Tel: **01856-874619**

*I*n the course of announcing his 1993 Budget to the House of Commons, the Chancellor of the UK Exchequer raised a glass of malt whisky to toast the success of the Scotch whisky industry; he then proceeded to raise the duty on wines but not on spirits. The whisky he waved before the nation watching on television was Highland Park 12-year-old.

Some of the Orkney islands seem to lie only feet above the water, scattered like great green carpets across the horizon; others loom blue-grey before you, hummocky and ice-rounded, with undoubted power and mass. Despite words to the contrary, Orkney does indeed have trees although they cluster in hollows and those nearest the prevailing winds are leafless and perished from the salt-spray they bear. Spaciousness and timelessness are what you feel in these landscapes, but the towns have their creature comforts. The little court of Orkney was said to be the most refined and elegant in the whole of Europe in the 14th century, and you can see what they meant with a glance at the Earl's Palace and St Magnus Cathedral.

The people of Orkney have been shaped by influences from all directions; as with any distinctive community, they are aware of their rich history and it is never a chore for them to talk about the uniqueness of their islands. Norse influences abound in islands that have been settled since 6000 BC; Orcadians went to Canada to work in the Hudson's Bay Company and married into the Cree Indian tribes there; certain residents of Westray are called Dons, descending, as they do, from a boatload of survivors from the Spanish Armada who were shipwrecked on its rocks.

Illicit distilling in Orkney was difficult to contain because of its remoteness. There was no stigma whatsoever associated with smuggling in the late 18th century because people were fed up with the extent to which the government heaped duty on to a wide range of goods to pay for the war with France. Tea, sugar and salt, in addition to whisky, were dutiable and the gin producers of the south were shamelessly protected by Parliament against prospective inroads by Scotch whisky. As a result, respectable people had no compunction about distillation on the quiet; indeed the provost (mayor) of Kirkwall and the government's own resident naval commander were among the leading smugglers in Orkney.

At the tail-end of the 18th century, none of the Orcadian distillers was permitted to export beyond the islands but extensive smuggling networks made it available in the Lowlands. Orkney whisky was of very high quality and Kirkwall provost, Thomas Traill, must have had excellent connections to enable him to transport his product. In 1805, the Excise blitzed the outer Orkney islands and seized many illicit stills so Traill played safe and opened a licensed brewery and distillery in Mill Street in Kirkwall. He worked with Magnus Eunson who had run an illicit still since 1798 on Kirkwall common land and it is thought that this was the original distillery on the Highland Park site. Eunson was said to have stored his full casks under the pulpit of a local church, away from the attention of the Excise officers. It must have been a fragrant atmosphere in which to sing hymns.

On one famous occasion, Eunson got wind of an impending raid. When the officers burst in, a funeral service was under way, with the coffin resting on supports covered with a white cloth. In case the covering might be raised to reveal the casks on which the coffin lay, the word, 'smallpox', whispered in an officer's ear, sent the party hurrying off without any further examination.

Two years after the new law of 1823 at last made distilling a viable business

proposition, Robert Borwick set up his Highland Park operation. Ironically, the buildings were owned by John Robertson, the Excise officer who had finally arrested Magnus Eunson a decade earlier. The main attraction of the site were the springs of crystal-clear water from a pool at Cattie Maggie's, and the Borwick family had a hand in running the distillery for the next 35 years. When James Borwick inherited the distillery in 1869, he quickly sold it on since he felt that ownership of such a

Left: The 'rabbit warren' of Skara Brae was, 5000 years ago, a complete prehistoric village.

Left: The Italian Chapel was built by Italian prisoners of War during World War II.

business would be inappropriate to his standing as a church minister.

In 1883, Sir Donald Currie visited Kirkwall with his liner, the Pembroke Castle, on its maiden voyage. He was greatly impressed by the quality of Highland Park whisky and took a quantity away when the voyage continued. By all accounts the King of Denmark and the Emperor of Russia, whom he entertained on board later, were equally enthusiastic about the whisky. More recently, Winston Churchill and Her Majesty the Queen have shown interest in the distillery and its whisky. The distillery is now owned by Highland Distilleries.

Most of the warehouses have traditional beaten-earth floors and they contain about 40,000 maturing casks. There are four stills. The floor maltings still in use at Highland Park are one of the few remaining in Scottish distilleries. About 600 tonnes of barley can be laid out on the V-shaped floors, where it is regularly turned to control heat build-up. The malt is dried in the kiln with a medium peating effect. The peat comes from the company's own moss at Hobbister Hill, near Scapa. It is cut in April, then stacked and dried over the summer for storing before use. The heather with which it is covered adds an important nuance to the final flavour.

The Whisky

Highland Park is full and resonant in flavour with smoky tones all through. It is not heavy, showing silky, slightly creamy texture. It is usually bottled at 12 years old and mainly 40% vol., but a 1967 vintage at 43% vol. was recently available. Independent bottlings range from eight- to 12-year-old and vintages go back to the 1950s.

Of interest nearby

• **Skara Brae** is a kind of prehistoric block of flats dating from 3000 BC and complete with storage boxes, furniture and wall-shelving, all made of stone.
• **Maes Howe** is a chambered tomb, regarded as the finest prehistoric architectural achievement in Europe. It is contemporary with Skara Brae and at the winter solstice sunlight shines directly down the passage to the chamber within the mound. The graffiti, scratched on the walls in runes by Viking tomb-robbers, date from the 12th century.
• **Stromness**, built with its shoulder to the sea, is an interesting little town. The museum is excellent and lies opposite the site of the old MacConnell distillery, founded in 1817 and silent from 1928.

Scapa Distillery

Location: **St. Ola, Kirkwall, Orkney KW15 1SE** • *Roads:* **A964**
Please telephone for information about visits • *Tel:* **01856-872071**

*B*eneath the waters of Scapa Flow still lie the hulks of the German war fleet from World War I, scuttled on the orders of von Reuter who was fed up with the slowness of the post-war repatriation negotiations. During World War II, convoys gathered here for escorting across the Atlantic and Scapa distillery was used as accommodation for naval ratings.

The distillery was opened in 1885 and embarked on a century of production involving few changes of ownership. It was silent for two years from 1934 and was owned for a time by the owners of Glen Scotia distillery in Campbeltown. Scapa was rebuilt in 1959 with further internal improvements made in 1978.

The water supply carries a considerable amount of peat from the Lingro Burn and local springs, as a result of which the barley it uses is left unpeated. The waterwheel that supplied power to the original distillery is still there but the maltings were taken out of use in the 1960s not long after the rebuilding of the distillery.

The distillery has a single pair of stills, which date from 1978 and one of them is of the Lomond type, a rare feature. It has a short, stubby top instead of the elongated conical heads customary in Scottish distilleries. An appealing aspect for hard-line traditionalists is that the whisky is made without the usual hi-tec automation. The distillate intended for bottling as a single malt is aged exclusively in ex-Bourbon casks - which is oakwood charred on the inside of the staves.

Left: One of the Churchill Barriers, linking the islands around Scapa Flow in the Orkneys.

The Whisky

Scapa is delicate, floral, salty and smooth textured. Elegant with slow-slide finish. It is bottles at 10 years, and 43% vol., although some 1979 was recently available.

Of interest nearby

• The **Churchill Barriers** are causeways built during World War II to link certain of the confetti of islands and keep out marauding German submarines.

Trail 2  North-East Coast

From Inverness to Macduff

Inverness skyline across the River Ness

Introduction

This trail leads along the north-eastern shoulder of Scotland where, although all of the distilleries are within the Highland category, some of the whiskies show greater robustness and depth due to their being matured in the breezy, salty air of the Moray Firth.

It is a gentle landscape of farms, old Royal Burghs, golf courses and castles, an area long and populously settled due to the fertility of the soil and the equable climate. The church was well established here a thousand years ago and the sophistication of the building by the 13th century advanced and refined.

Above: Inverness, the capital of the Highlands, has grown up at the point where the River Ness empties into the Moray Firth.

Royal Brackla Distillery

Location: **Nairn, Morayshire**

Nairn is one of the driest and sunniest spots in Britain, proof that the north of Scotland is not, as many people think, a permanently rain-swept upland. Nairn is a resort with a championship golf course, fine beaches and a harbour built by Thomas Telford. The town does straggle along the shore for some way; so much so, in fact, that King James VI of Scotland and I of England declared that his subjects living at one end did not understand the language of those who lived at the other. Nairn was also the seat of the Thane of Cawdor and the birthplace of James Grant, who accompanied Speke on his expeditions to find the source of the River Nile. He even reminisced fondly about drinking Brackla whisky in a letter home to his sister from the 1860 journey.

The distillery was founded by a Captain Fraser in 1812 at the height of the illicit whisky monopoly. He complained that he was surrounded by people who drank nothing but whisky yet he could not sell 100 gallons in a year. The distillery is one

of only three ever entitled to the 'Royal' epithet. In Brackla's case, it was bestowed as a result of King William IV's particular liking for the whisky and it was called 'The King's Own Whisky'. Brackla was used in the making of the very first blended whiskies assembled from malts and grains, a

Left: A wall of windows shows off the stills at Royal Brackla – even when they are being cleaned!

2

procedure developed by Edinburgh merchant, Andrew Usher. The distillery remained in the hands of the Fraser family until the end of the century.

In 1966 the floor maltings were closed and the single pair of stills became two. In the course of that reconstruction programme, most of the older buildings were demolished, although the modern plant is attractively situated looking on to the distillery pond.

The Whisky

This is a big, intense malt with a fair degree of smoke and sweetness. It is bottled by United Distillers at 10 years and 43% vol. and an unaged single malt at 40% vol. but 1976 and 1972 are available elsewhere.

Of interest nearby

• **Cawdor Castle**, supposedly where Macbeth murdered King Duncan. The present castle's foundations only date from the 1400s but there was an earlier keep on the same site.

• **Fishertown Museum** on King Street tells the story of the town's fishing industry.

• **Fort George**, constructed to keep the clans in check after Culloden, was highly successful in the sense that it never fired a shot in anger. The rampart is a mile long and encloses an area of 42 acres.

Above: Cawdor Castle has become a well-known name because it is featured in Shakespeare's Macbeth. The castle we can see today dates back nearly 600 years, but there is evidence of earlier building on the same site.

Dallas Dhu Distillery

Location: **Forres, Morayshire**
Roads: **Off the A940, one mile in direction of Rafford**
Tel: **01309-672802**

---

*T*he town of Forres may well be the 'Varris' that appeared on Roman maps of the district 2,000 years ago. Be that as it may, there certainly was a ninth-century Royal residence in the town and its layout today is mediaeval, with streets converging on the market place and narrow lanes linking them. Most of the old town buildings are 17th and 18th century and display the distinctive Scottish architectural feature of crow-stepped gables.

Forres had two distilleries in full production at the beginning of the 1980s but, unfortunately, neither maintained the same status into the 1990s. Benromach closed in 1983 and Dallas Dhu went not long afterwards. Yet the latter lives on, fully rigged out and in production mode, as a living museum. It is open to visitors, its whisky is still available (although dwindling all the time), incomparably expert ex-distillery

2

Above: Forres is a quiet Morayshire town, particularly colourful in spring.

workers are often among those who show you round and you see the place exactly as it was when it was in production – all that is missing is that it does not actually distil whisky any more.

Dallas Dhu is such a perfect Highland distillery that, uniquely, it became the responsibility of the Scottish Historic Buildings and Monuments Department and is now officially a protected Ancient Monument. Appropriately, it is one of the distilleries designed by the talented Elgin architect, Charles Doig, much of whose work can still be seen around the Highlands today. It may even be he who invented the shapely rooftop pagoda-head kiln-ventilators that distinguish distilleries so readily.

Dallas Dhu was completed in 1899. It was one of several distilleries located on the estate of a local laird, Alexander Edward, and the following year he handed Dallas Dhu over to the proprietors of Roderick Dhu, one of the popular whisky brands of the day. It was a prime site for distilling with water from the Altyre Burn and local barley, for long one of the best growing districts in Scotland. It was near the Highland Railway's main line and the distillery had its own siding.

Due to the two World Wars, the depression and a fire that destroyed the stillhouse in 1939, production was an on/off affair until 1947 but the distillery played its part in the whisky boom of the following 30 years. One of the reasons

Dallas Dhu kept its Victorian form was the limited water supply. Had there been more of it, much of what we see today, both inside and out, might well have been removed and replaced in pursuit of expanded production and efficiency.

It is a delight to walk round the floors and buildings being able to see in place and in sequence all of the machinery and equipment that is only partly present elsewhere. The barley-loft, the malting floor, the kiln, the malt mill and all the way through to the stillhouse and warehouses – they are all there.

Electricity did not reach Dallas Dhu until the 1950s and the waterwheel, driven by the overflow from the worm-tub, still contributed to the power pool into the 1970s. There is a single pair of stills, looking as if they could get under way at any moment.

The Whisky

Dallas Dhu had some complexity and, although not quite a 'big' whisky, it had a silky, glyceral texture and botanical/floral bite. The final distillations were in 1983, so batches continue to crop up. Some 18-year-old and 1978 were recently available.

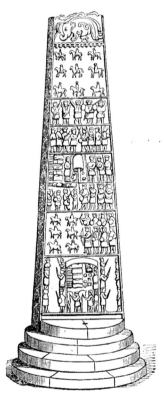

Of interest nearby

• **Sueno's Stone** is a 23-foot carved Pictish upright stone dating from the ninth century. It commemorates a battle and the sculpting is extraordinary. Apart from some Ogam inscriptions and their broch towers, all that remains of the Picts, who shared Scotland with the Scots themselves from the third to the ninth centuries and simply disappeared, are these intricately carved stones which are scattered around the Highlands.

Left: Sueno's Stone or Pillar, in the town of Forres, is thought to commemorate a battle with the Danes, but there does not seem to be any convincing explanation for the elephant at the top of the carving.

2

Glenburgie-Glenlivet Distillery

Location: **Alves, by Forres, Morayshire IV36 0QU**
Roads: **Off A95 east of Forres**
Please telephone for information about visiting
Tel: **01343-850258**

Not far from Forres is the village of Alves with its Knock Hill where Macbeth is said to have met 'the weird sisters'. The York Tower on its crown looks pleasingly Gothic but is, in fact, really quite recent. Alves is also the location of Glenburgie distillery, one of the main constituents of Ballantine's whisky blends.

There are indications that there was a distillery on the site by 1810 but official records state that William Paul began production in 1829 and the distillery was named Kinflat. It had fallen into disuse by 1870 but was revived in 1878, for the first time under the name of Glenburgie. In 1928, Margaret Nicol became one of the latterday lady managers of a Highland distillery and progressed to be her employer's divisional secretary for malt distilleries until she retired in 1958.

For a while it produced two different whiskies by the installation, in 1958, of two Lomond stills. These were used to make Glencraig malt whisky, named for a former director of the parent company's Highland distilleries. If there is any Glencraig still in existence it will never be added to since the Lomond stills were subsequently displaced by a second pair of the Glenburgie type.

Water has tended to be in short supply at Glenburgie. Attempts were made to locate extra sources by sinking boreholes but without success. The problem is slightly alleviated by retaining the cooling water and pumping it back into the distillery dam for continuous recycling. There is also a cooling tower for storage. Vestiges of the original distillery offices and warehousing have survived the successive rebuilding work over the years. The floor maltings were utilised until 1958. A single pair of stills was used for the main Glenburgie production, which was normally kept separate from the spirit made in the Lomond stills and destined for Glencraig.

The Whisky

Glenburgie is a succulently aromatic malt. It is very rich with touches of peat and a background of heather flower. 'Official' single malt bottlings are infrequent but the independents seem to have no trouble in coming up with some choice on the matter. Eight-, 13- and 28-year-old, as well as 1960, 1966 and 1968 vintages, have recently been available.

Glencraig has more gravitas from its Lomond origins, with oily, jammy warmth and considerable fruit presence. It is much scarcer than Glenburgie with some 1970 lately in circulation.

Left: Duffus Castle at Alves was built some 700 years ago. It stands on a mound, surrounded by the ditch that formed part of its fortification.

Of interest nearby

• **Duffus Castle** was the original family seat of the de Moravia family, Norman incomers who were given lands in the wake of the Norman Conquest of England. They made their mark and gave their name to the county of Morayshire. Duffus Castle is, not surprisingly, a Norman motte-and-bailey castle dating from the late 1200s and is unique in its having an encircling ditch.

• **Gordonstoun School**, favoured for the education of successive male generations of the British Royal Family (and a sprinkling of distillers' sons), is a fine house in spacious grounds near Duffus. It is now co-educational.

Miltonduff Distillery

Location: **Elgin, Morayshire IV30 3TQ**
Roads: **Off the B9010 south of Elgin**
Days: **Mon – Thurs • All visits by appointment**
Tel: **01343-547433**

Elgin had gained and lost considerable nobility and sophistication long before Columbus crossed to the New World; its cathedral, begun in the 1100s, showed soaring grace before its destruction, and the town was a favoured Royal Burgh in the 1200s. Part of a 1687 carved stone in the cathedral graveyard reads, 'If lyfe were a thing that monie could buy the poor could not live and the rich could not die.' Elegant buildings from the 17th and 18th centuries scattered here and there give a pleasing serendipity touch to town walks. Some of the best barley in Britain is cropped in the surrounding fields.

Pluscarden Priory dates from 1236 and over the centuries on New Year's Day the Benedictine abbots used to bless the waters of the Black Burn where Miltonduff distillery now stands. It is not out of the question that the production of aqua vitae was carried out there by the monks, particularly since religious orders in Ireland and south-west Scotland seem to have been guardians of the secrets of distillation since the Dark Ages. Moreover, the distillery buildings were once a meal-mill run by the monks at the priory.

In the years before Miltonduff was built in 1824, wisps of smoke regularly rose from hollows all over the surrounding glen, each the signature of a fire boiling an illicit still. The distillery was one of the new generation of such businesses born after the 1823 Excise Act. In the 1860s it was owned for a time by James Grant who owned Highland Park in Orkney. In 1895, it was extended and it may well have been then that the stone upon which the abbot knelt during his ceremonies was

built into the support wall of one of the stills. The Catholic Church was given a further brief direct interest in Miltonduff; in 1900 the Elgin parish was bequeathed a share of the ownership, but these were difficult times in whisky making and the stock was sold on soon after. The distillery was substantially rebuilt in 1974/75 and is now the largest of the distilleries owned by the Allied Distillers group. 'Duff' was added to the name when the land on which the distillery stood was bought by the Duff family, the Dukes of Fife. Miltonduff has kept alive the agricultural dimension to distilling that goes back to the days when whisky making was a part-time perk for farmers. The company still owns and runs the farms around the distillery.

In 1964 a pair of Lomond stills was installed, the spirit of which was named Mosstowie, but they were removed in 1981. There are now three pairs shaped in the traditional Miltonduff configuration. Miltonduff used to be triple-distilled, a final vestige of the old routine when stills were a little less efficient than they are today.

The Whisky

Petal-fragrant, sweetly sappy gentle style of malt with a little smoke and a touch of vanilla. Standard issue is 12-year-old at 43% vol. and there is also some 13-year-old in circulation. Miltonduff is the main malt in Ballantine's blended whiskies.

Of interest nearby

• **Pluscarden Abbey** mouldered after the Reformation but was revived in 1948. Promotion from priory to abbey status took place in 1973.

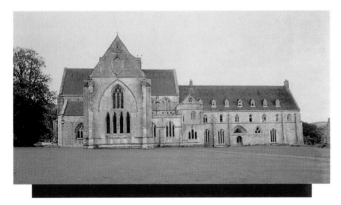

Left: Pluscarden Priory was founded in 1236 by Benedictine monks. It is likely that they held many of the secrets of the distillation process.

Glen Moray Distillery

Location: **Elgin, Morayshire IV30 1YE**
Roads: **Bruceland Road, off Whittet Drive at edge of town**
Seasons: **All year •** *Hours:* **By appoinment, Mon – Fri; please ring ahead
Group bookings, max 12 • No reception centre or shop**
Tel: **01343-542577**

*T*he old road into Elgin passes through the grounds of Glen Moray distillery just below the Gallowcrook Hill where executions were carried out until the end of the 17th century. This was an important road in times now gone and many famous people have passed along it. King Duncan was carried to Elgin to die, wounded by Macbeth after the Battle of Burghead; Bonnie Prince Charlie and his tired army tramped through on the way to the Jacobites' final catastrophe at Culloden, pursued by the criminally remorseless Cumberland and his Hanoverian forces; Boswell and Dr. Johnson must have noticed the tension between locals and soldiers stationed at nearby Fort George, when they trundled into town less than 30 years later.

A brewery, built in 1815, was converted in 1897 as part of the distillery-building bandwagon of the time in the Highlands. This one was named Glen Moray and it made fine whisky but times were difficult and it could not escape closure in 1910.

In 1920 both Aberlour and Glen Moray distilleries were put up for sale and Macdonald & Muir decided to buy one of them. They left it to the manager of their Glenmorangie distillery to make the choice, and he opted for Glen Moray. Production continued with the set-up as it reached the new owners until the post-war boom in demand for whisky made investment in its expansion and doubling of

Above: From the battlements of Fort George, which dates back to 1769, there is a clear view across the Moray Firth.

capacity a good idea. Distillery staff know a good life when they see one and the last two managers at Glen Moray worked there for 47 and 44 years respectively. The water is drawn from the River Lossie on whose bank the distillery stands.

Glen Moray is square in plan, forming a courtyard with buildings on all four sides – the classic layout of the time for Highland farms and, by extension, the distilleries that grew from them. The floor maltings were replaced in 1958 by a Saladin Box system but it was only used for about 20 years before the distillery went over to specialist malt suppliers. The old steam engine that formerly powered the machinery is now in storage. There are four stills, two very new (1992) and two from the 1970s.

The Whisky

Glen Moray shows fruit and spice with vanilla laced through it from the American oak casks in which the spirit matures. Sweet, too, with warmth and some richness. The customary bottlings are at 12, 15 and 17 years and 40% vol. and the company also do special editions with 1960, 1962, 1966 and 1967, all at 43% vol., currently available. Few casks are released for independent bottling.

• Moving on •

This North Coast Trail now heads into the town of Elgin which provides the opportunity for a break, a snack or a walk before travelling on. A worthwhile visit could be made to Gordon & MacPhail, one of the main independent whisky specialists, whose one-off bottlings make available to consumers a much greater scatter of ages and styles of whisky than are released by the distilleries themselves. The shop, not surprisingly, has an in-depth selection of whiskies.

Glenglassaugh Distillery

Location: **Portsoy, Banffshire**
Roads: **Off the A98 two miles west of Portsoy**
Please telephone for information about visiting • *Tel:* 0261-42367

Glenglassaugh stands on raised, open ground near the sea and near the pretty fishing village of Portsoy. In Napoleonic times, smugglers used to gather in the Star Inn in North High Street; even then it was already a century old. In the 18th century a pink and green serpentine stone was mined here, which went into fine houses all over Britain and Europe. Several chimneypieces in the Palais de Versailles are made from Portsoy marble, the latter so-called because Lord Boyne was able to have imports of foreign marble to Britain banned to protect sales of the Portsoy stone that came from his estates. Boyne Castle, east of town, was the home of Mary Beaton, one of Mary Queen of Scots' *Four Marys* in the old song.

Glenglassaugh was founded in 1875 and was bought by present owners, Highland Distilleries, during the 1890s. The distillery was in production only for very short bursts during the period 1907-1960, amounting to a meagre four or five years in all. It was rebuilt in 1960 to an advanced design for the time and has stayed in production until the present except for a silent period in the late 1980s. The buildings are functional and unremarkable in appearance.

Peat used to be cut from the Crombie moss nearby and the distillery grew its own barley on an 80-acre farm. The fast flow of the River Glassaugh was utilised from the outset and the distillery was entirely water-powered for a long time.

The distillery has only ever had a single pair of stills but it succeeded in doubling production capacity simply by installing new stills of double the previous size. These have 'boil pots' on the necks – round bulges that create a kind of reflux, to yield lighter spirit.

The Whisky

Glenglassaugh has taut, smooth texture and a quiet, almost closed understatement of fruit and cream flavour. Teasingly distant, balanced and a little earthy, perhaps from the seashore winds. It is bottled at 12 years and 40/43% vol., and is used in Famous Grouse, Cutty Sark and other blends.

Macduff Distillery

Location: **Banff, Banffshire**
Roads: **By Banff golf course east of town**
Please telephone for information about visiting • *Tel:* 01261-812612

*T*he town of Banff has a long trading pedigree. It goes back to the 12th century when it was one of the Hanseatic League towns and had a fleet which traded in the Mediterranean and the Baltic. Then herring fishing boomed and faded, and now Banff is in semi-retirement with its fine buildings and gardens all around and pleasure craft bobbing in its harbour.

Macduff on the other side of the Deveron estuary was a spa town for a while but its larger harbour inherited the herring fleet from Banff and fishing is its mainstay. The town is the location of Macduff, a rare malt distillery in that its name is not used by the proprietors for the bottled whisky that it produces. The official name for the single malt from Macduff is Glen Deveron, called after the river on whose bank is sits. The Macduff name is used, however, by independent bottlers.

The distillery is modern, having been completed in 1960. The setting beside both river and coast is most attractive but the distillery itself is rather severe. Macduff started with a single pair of stills in 1960. Two years later a third on its own was added, then, in 1968 a fourth, making two pairs. The stills were lagged, thereby making a considerable saving in heating costs compared to other distilleries who prefer the glamorous colour of the copper to be seen. Macduff has its own cooperage. The Tun room and still house were renovated in 1990,

2

Left: The warehouses at Macduff are purpose-built, but barrels are stacked in a traditional manner. Below: A trip to the picturesque fishing village of Fraserburgh rounds off the trail. The town is half way between Banff and Peterhead, the end of the third trail.

The Whisky

Glen Deveron (and Macduff when the bottler is other than the proprietors) is clean, fresh and very fruity, malty-smooth rather than old'n'mellowed smooth. Sometimes sherry shows through. The style is very appropriate to being drunk young, which is how Italians like malts (the proprietors also own Martini). Glen Deveron is 12 years old, with a five-year-old version for export mainly to Italy. Strength is 40/43% vol., depending on destination. Macduff from independents has recently been available as a 1975 vintage and a 14-year-old. The malt is used in William Lawson blends.

Left: High on the cliffs overlooking Cruden bay stands Slains Castle. The gabled façade hints at its former splendour.

Of interest nearby

• **Duff House** is a beautiful Georgian Baroque mansion, designed in 1735 by William Adam. It has had a number of roles – including a POW camp – and is being prepared to house part of the National Galleries of Scotland collections.

• **Banff Castle** is also a William Adam house (1750) and has connections with General San Martin, liberator of Argentina, who lived in Banff during his exile. There is apparently a square in Buenos Aires called Plaza Banff, which acknowledges the hospitality he received in those days.

• **Slains Castle**, seat of the Earls of Erroll at Cruden Bay, was the inspiration for the vampire count's Transylvanian castle in Bram Stoker's novel Dracula. An early draft of the book had Count Dracula arriving in Britain at Slains, though this was subsequently changed to Whitby in Yorkshire

• M o v i n g   o n •

It is well worth while continuing on via Pennan and Fraserburgh to end the trail at Peterhead. Pennan is very pretty and secluded, and the bays and caves were long used by smugglers, not just of whisky. The cliff village of Pennan was the location of the Bill Forsyth movie, *Local Hero*.

Fraserburgh was briefly a university town in the 1590s when students moved away from Aberdeen during a cholera epidemic. However, almost everyone returned to their old college when it was safe to do so and the idea was abandoned. Fraserburgh Castle dates from the 1570s and in 1787 Scotland's first lighthouse was installed in its top storey. Twenty whale-oil lamps originally supplied the light but it is now fully automatic.

Trail 3  East Highlands

From Brechin to Peterhead

Introduction

From Brechin in Angus we head north through gentle hills and valleys peppered with comfortable estates and farmland. As we progress, the hills become more substantial and the rivers a little faster. Although there are still farms, fields and large houses, mountainsides become visible from farther off and mansions become castles. Stone-built villages abound, sometimes austere, sometimes flower-bedecked, always practical.

The distilleries we encounter all produce malt whisky of the Highland type.

Above: Dunnottar Castle occupies an imposing position on volcanic rocks outside Stonehaven. The morning mists clear to reveal extensive ruins, approached by a steep path.

3

Glencadam Distillery

Location: **Brechin, Angus**
Roads: **Half a mile to the east of Brechin** • *Seasons:* **All year except July**
Hours: **2pm - 4pm, Mon - Thur; all visits by appointment**
Group bookings, max 10 • *Tel:* **01356-622217** *Fax:* **01356-624926**

Brechin's cathedral dates from 1150 and the unique Round Tower (there is one other like it in Scotland at Abernethy) was the work of settler Irish clergy in 1012. The town used to have two distilleries but North Port was closed in 1983 and recently demolished.

Glencadam was founded in 1825 and although it had a high turnover in owners over the years, this seems to have indicated continued interest in working it. Certainly there were no lengthy periods during which Glencadam was out of production. It was acquired by Hiram Walker in 1954 (later Allied Domecq) and modernised in 1959.

The distillery has a single pair of stills, which are distinctive by the way the lyne-arms at the top rise as they taper away from the necks; most stills tend to have lyne-arms that are horizontal or descend as they conduct the vapours away from the boil.

The Whisky

Glencadam has good body and resonance but is more sweet and fruit than smoke or peat. There are flashes of the latter but this is a summery kind of malt. No official bottlings are released, most of the make going into the Ballantine blends, but the

Above: At Brechin Station, steam railway enthusiasts can take a scenic trip down towards the coast. The line ends at Bridge of Dun, close to a fine bird sanctuary, Montrose Basin.

independents offer several, all of them over 20 years old and including a 1974 vintage.

Of interest nearby

• The **Caledonian Railway** has taken over old Brechin station and runs between there and Bridge of Dun near Montrose. Special steam days are part of the year-round programmes.

• **A Heritage Trail** can be followed through the 12th-century and mediaeval parts of Brechin.

• **North Port Distillery** was, until its recent demolition, Brechin's other whisky-producer. Its whisky can still be found.

• **Lochside Distillery** further up the trail at Montrose is a converted brewery, which has produced both malt and grain whisky in its time.

• **Glenesk Folk Museum** recounts the local way of life over a number of different periods in the past.

• The **Lifeboat Station** at Montrose was the first to be established by the Royal National Lifeboat Institute, and the first boat was launched in 1869. Visitors welcome.

• The **House of Dun** is an elegant Palladian mansion designed by William Adam, father of Robert and James. Many of Adam senior's country houses are located in the north-east of Scotland.

Fettercairn Distillery

Location: **Fettercairn, Laurencekirk, Kincardineshire AB30 1YB**
Roads: **5 miles inland off A94** • *Seasons:* **May – September**
Hours: **10am – 4.30pm, Mon – Sat (last tour 4pm)**
Group bookings, max 40; please telephone
Reception centre, shop and audio–visual presentation
Tel: **015613–40205**

*A*t the beginning of the 19th century, the village of Fettercairn had one surgeon, five flaxdressers, seven shopkeepers, 10 millers and 50 weavers. There were also plenty of distillers but they could not be detailed in this contemporary description of the village because they were all illicit operators working on the upper, more remote slopes of Cairn-o'-Mount nearby.

When licensed distilling became more feasible after 1823, Fettercairn distillery's founders came, if not in from the cold, certainly down from higher up the mountain where they had been part of the smuggling fraternity. A new distillery was built in 1824 and respectability was more openly enjoyed. It was situated a couple of miles below the old site and on the Fasque estate, which was bought in 1830 by the father of William Gladstone who later served several terms as British Prime Minister. Fettercairn whisky was used in the Buchanan and Johnnie Walker blended whisky brands that had become so popular by the end of the century.

The distillery, converted from an old cornmill in 1824, was among the first flush of licensed operations that followed the watershed Act of the preceding year. It was rebuilt after a fire in 1887 and then was silent from 1926 until the outbreak of World War II. During that period, it had come close to being dismantled since a buyer

Above: Fasque house, the childhood home of William Gladstone, is set in extensive grounds near Laurencekirk. The kitchens and sculleries remain as they were when Gladstone's father bought the estate in 1829.

could not be found. In the event Joseph Hobbs (see Ben Nevis) bought the distillery, although no production could take place before the outbreak of World War II. Fettercairn now belongs to Whyte & Mackay. There are two pairs of stills which have reflux fixtures fitted to their rather straight necks. The warehouses contain about 25,000 casks of whisky at different stages of maturity, some going back to 1939.

The Whisky

Old Fettercairn is the official name for the whisky. It is lightly peated but the water used to make it is also peaty so it emerges as a well-textured malt with creamy, fine feel and medium weight. Some smoke, spice, vanilla lacing and a nutty/malty tone all the way through. The standard issue is 10 years old and 40/43% vol., with rare offerings from the independents. It is used in the Whyte & Mackay blend.

Of interest nearby

• **Fasque** was the estate bought by the Gladstones and where William Gladstone grew up. The large house contains contains a wealth of 'Upstairs Downstairs' Victoriana.

Royal Lochnagar Distillery

Location: **Crathie, Ballater, Aberdeenshire AB35 5TB**
Roads: **Off the B976 or from A93 Aberdeen – Braemar**
Seasons: **All year, 10am – 5pm, Mon – Fri; also Easter – October, same
times Sat and 11am – 4pm, Sun • Group bookings by appointment
Reception centre, shop, coffee shop, exhibition, (non-producing) illicit
still and audio-visual • *Tel:* 013397-42273**

*I*t is one thing for the new neighbours to drop in to visit – quite another when they
turn out to be Queen Victoria, husband, children and lady-in-waiting. This is what
happened one evening in 1848 when John Begg looked out of the window and saw
the little gaggle of figures walking up the driveway towards his house. He lived at
Crathie by the River Dee and the Royal Family were about to buy the Balmoral
estate next door to the new distillery, which Begg had built just three years earlier.

When the Royals arrived for their first stay at Balmoral, Begg had handed in a
note inviting them to 'see round his works', rather impudently hinting that if they
did not get there by 6pm the following evening, they would miss seeing the
distillery in operation. No question of extending the routine to accommodate Her
Majesty – be there or you miss it, he seemed, perhaps ingenuously, to be saying.

The Queen and Prince Albert saw round, had the process explained and dipped
their fingers in the new spirit to taste it while the little princes chased each other in
and out of the rows of casks. Some mature whisky was taken from bond for
sampling and, when Prince Albert seemed about to drink it in a single gulp, Begg

Left: Lochnagar Distillery became known as 'Royal Lochnagar' in the middle of the 19th century, after a visit from Queen Victoria. Below: An early advertisement for John Begg's Lochnagar whisky.

quickly reminded him that it was cask-strength and very strong. Subsequently Begg was permitted to describe his distillery as 'Royal' Lochnagar and he was appointed, by Royal warrant, 'Distiller to Her Majesty'. Over the years, further Royal Warrants followed. Sending that note was the best thing for business Begg ever did.

Scottish children try to trick each other by asking how deep Lochnagar is, the catch being that it is not a loch but a mountain. It not very high (3789 feet/1155m) but it is bulky and dominates the smiling, tidy countryside below.

The Royal connection has meant a string of famous visitors to the distillery, many of them British prime ministers taking an hour or so off between meetings with the monarch of the day at Balmoral.

The first licensed Lochnagar distillery was set up on the north side of the river in 1826 by a former illicit distiller. That operation was burned down by fellow smugglers aggrieved at one of their number 'going legit', but it was rebuilt, so that in 1845 when Begg built his distillery on the south bank he called it New Lochnagar. The north-bank distillery had closed by 1860 and Lochnagar continued to prosper although the Abergeldie Estates consistently refused to sell the distillery the grounds it occupied, preferring to see value being added to their land through the erection of extensions and new buildings necessary for Lochnagar's continuing development.

The distillery became a trust for Begg's grandchildren, then a limited company, and was rebuilt in 1906. In 1916 it was sold to DCL. Most of the 1906 structure disappeared in the next rebuilding in 1963, although the malt-barn and the kiln, out of use since 1966, still survive, the latter reflecting evocatively in the distillery pond on bright, windless days.

Lighting was by paraffin lamp until 1949 and power was by waterwheel well into the 1960s. Most unusual are two cast-iron steeping vessels, which are rectangular in shape (these are almost universally cylindrical elsewhere). Lochnagar has a lot of storage capacity for raw materials so that distilling can continue when the distillery is snowed in. There is a single pair of stills but they are unusual in having lyne-arms (the tapering conical top sections) which dip downwards; most others are more or less horizontal. Each still has its own worm-tub – cast iron instead of wood – to condense the spirit.

Right: Braemar is the setting for the annual Royal Highland Gathering, held in the late summer. As well as bands of pipers, there are traditional Scottish sports such as tossing the caber.

The Whisky

Royal Lochnagar has a malty, raisiny, medium-weight flavour with some spice, oakiness and smokiness; well balanced and pleasing, but uncomplicated. Very approachable, zesty, sweetish but checked by alcoholic nip. The very expensive boxed old Lochnagar is richer, sherried and mellow.

Of interest nearby

• **Braemar** is best known for its Highland Games but the village has its own distinct identity. The Jacobite standard was raised here at the start of the 1715 Rebellion against the Crown. Braemar proper was created in 1870 by two tiny settlements, one Catholic and one Presbyterian (Protestant), coming together to live as a single community.

Above: Queen Victoria bought the Balmoral Estate to provide a holiday retreat for herself and her family. Towers and turrets give the building a romantic, fairy-tale atmosphere.

• The **Braemar Royal Highland Gathering** takes place in September in a beautiful natural amphitheatre. It is a colourful and noisy spectacle of pipe bands, Highland dancing, tossing the caber, throwing events, tug o' war, athletics and competitors clad in a hundred different tartans. It is merely the best-known event, however, and if you cannot get a ticket, two or three Highland Games are held every week from May to September in towns and villages all over the country.

• The grounds of **Balmoral Castle** are open to visitors when the Royal Family is not there. Normally they only appear in September for a holiday so there are plenty of opportunities to see the gardens in the course of the summer.

• **Crathie Church** is where the Royal Family worships while staying at Balmoral. Sunday morning outside the church is a good time to glimpse them, plus any guests, arriving and departing - if you can beat the crowds, that is. The first of five churches on the site dates from the ninth century and the remains of the mediaeval one can be seen in Crathie's old churchyard.

• **Dunnottar Castle** has a quite spectacular setting on a 160-foot-high plug of rock on the coast south of Stonehaven. It is a dramatic ruin after many sieges and was occupied by Cromwell in the 1650s. Cannons from Dunnottar were used by the Jacobite army in the 1715 Rebellion. The French Cognac brand, Otard, was founded by a family member who followed Bonnie Prince Charlie into exile in 1746; one of the Otards held a wedding reception in the ruins some years ago. In 1990, Mel Gibson and Glenn Close shot location scenes at Dunnottar for Zeffirelli's film version of *Hamlet*.

Glen Garioch Distillery

Location: **Old Meldrum, Aberdeenshire**
Roads: **On the A947 in the village**
Not open to visitors

*T*he name is pronounced 'Glen-gheery', as you may find out if you ask directions to the distillery. Old Meldrum is rich farmland and abounds with fields of cereal crops; the district used to be known as the granary of Aberdeenshire.

The distillery was founded in 1797 and had a succession of owners including Sanderson's (who used the malt in their Vat 69 blend), gin distillers Booth's and DCL, who closed it in 1968 because they said there was not enough water for distillation. A forerunner of the present owners bought it two years later, dug a new well in a neighbouring field and production started once more. The exterior of Glen Garioch is most attractive, a small-scale cluster of mellowed stone buildings, usually with pagoda heads, making up a well-preserved exterior. The floor maltings are still in use and supply just on half of the required amount of malt. The rest is brought in from outside maltsters.

Peat was cut from from local Pitsligo Moss for the malt drying. The peat was burned under the malt for about four hours to endow the correct degree of flavour for Glen Garioch and the drying is completed by gas-firing. A third still was added to the original pair in 1973, and then a fourth. One of the wash stills is twice the size of the other and the two spirit stills. Sadly, the distillery is closed at time of writing (1996) and is seeking new ownership.

The Whisky

Glen Garioch has considerable elegance as well as a fine, smoky persona. The peatiness is balanced rather than pungent and merges well with good flowery malt and there is excellent, medium-bodied smoothness in the finish. Owners Morrison Bowmore produce a 15 and 21-year-old as well as various 'vintage' bottlings and 21 year old ceramics. The make is used in other group blends such as Rob Roy, and Clan Roy.

Of interest nearby

• **Fyvie Castle** has five fine towers and represents perhaps the peak of the Scottish

Above left: The floor maltings at Glen Garioch. Above right: Drawing a sample to check that the whisky is maturing according to expectation. Left: Clean, symmetrical lines, turrets and towers make Fyvie a fine example of Baronial architecture.

Baronial style of architecture. The armour collection is rather special and there is a fine clutch of Raeburn paintings. Fyvie also has a **Donkey Sanctuary**.
• A working **Oatmeal Mill** at Alford offers conducted tours twice-weekly by appointment (tel: 09755-62209).
• **Grampian Transport Museum**, also at Alford, has a snowplough, a steam tricycle, an armoured car, a tram car and a car collection. There is also go-kart hire on a road circuit.

Ardmore Distillery

Location: **Kennethmont, Aberdeenshire**
Roads: **Off B9002 at Knockandy Hill**
Please telephone for information about visits • *Tel:* 01464-3213

*T*he Leith family were lairds of this settled, beguiling district of pasture and crop-fields. Their elegant seat at Leith Hall displays a wealth of material and artefacts from successive generations of the family and the grounds still have their unique stables and an 18th-century 'fridge', an ice-house.

Close by, since the turn of the century, Kennethmont has had its very own distillery. Ardmore went up in 1899 just as the world of whisky was falling down amidst the collapse of the Pattison company. However, it was built by Teacher's to guarantee supplies of malt whisky for their own blending requirements; their Highland Cream brand had gone on the market in 1884 and was doing well. The distillery, one of the largest in Scotland, was acquired by Allied Breweries in 1976, who have since evolved into Allied Distillers Ltd.

Malting with a Saladin Box system was continued until 1976, but when capacity was doubled (for the second time since 1955), the distillery went over to heavily peated malt from central suppliers. There are now four pairs of stills, all of which are coal-fired (now very unusual) and the inevitable soot that lands everywhere has given the still house the appearance of an old-time distillery although the building is modern.

The Whisky

Ardmore is full, round and a little unctuous due to its sweetness but, thanks to its lightly peated malt specification, is not notably smoky. It is complex, nonetheless, with light toffee and tar from the sherry and a sappy, dry astringency at the edges. Ardmore makes a splendid blending malt and no official regular self whisky is bottled, although an occasional 15-year-old is released. Independents sometimes have 12- to 20-year-olds and a 1977 vintage has recently been seen on lists. Ardmore, with Glendronach (*qv*), is used in the blending of Teacher's Highland Cream.

3

Glendronach Distillery

Location: **Forgue, Aberdeenshire AB54 6DB**
Roads: **On the B9001 off A97 Huntly-Banff**
Hours: **Tours at 10am and 2pm, Mon - Fri; by appointment only**
Group bookings, max 100 • Reception centre and shop
Tel: **01466 730202** • *Fax:* **01466-730313**

*T*he distillery is set among the gentle, green slopes of the Valley of Forgue in Aberdeenshire's 'castle country'. It is rural and peaceful although the colony of rooks in the great, mature trees around the distillery regularly create a breach of the peace. It was precisely such noisy commotion that made the rooks of 200 years ago useful allies of illicit distillers; they always gave warning of anyone, Excise officers included, who approached unannounced.

At Glendronach all of the auxiliary preparation for distilling continues to be done in the traditional ways – it has its own floor maltings and pagoda-headed malt-kiln. Fermentation vessels are still made of wood, the stills are coal-fired and the distillery even grows some of its own barley locally. The local lairds are the Dukes of Gordon and it was the 5th Duke who persuaded the London government that fair licensing was the best way to beat whisky smuggling. The 1823 Excise Act was a direct result of his commonsense approach to the problem. The distillery was founded in 1826 by a consortium of farmers and businessmen. In 1881 it was acquired and enlarged by Walter Scott, who had worked at Teaninich for a while. In 1920, Charles Grant, son of the founder of Glenfiddich distillery, bought Glendronach and it remained in the Grant family until it was sold to Teacher in 1960.

The Dronac burn, whose name has been taken for the whisky and the distillery, flows through the grounds. With so many of the traditional practices still being followed and the buildings themselves so little changed, the 'feel' both inside and out is most satisfying. The earth floors in the warehouses hold moisture, absorbing some of the excess from the air in wet weather and releasing it during extended hot spells in summertime. The floor maltings are still in use and provide a proportion (about 15 per cent) of the malt needed for production. Glendronach is lightly peated. There are two pairs of stills, which are heated by naked flames from coal fires.

The water for production comes from local springs and barley is grown on the company's own farms located in the district around the distillery.

The Whisky

Glendronach used to be available in two official editions – the Original, from plain and sherry casks, and a 100 per cent sherry-aged version. There is now a single official edition – the Traditional, at 12 years old and 40/43% vol. – which seeks to combine the merits of both styles by changing the proportions previously used for the original. The new 'recipe' is still a sherried style but casks that have been filled once, or even twice, before with whisky are used to let other aromas and flavours come through the sherry.

Certainly, both the creamy oakiness and the toasty toffee of respectively plain and sherry casks now show distinctly, and the elegant malt and smoke that were common to both before shine through in excellent balance. Texture is big and smooth. Occasional official special editions are released, such as the recent 18-year-old (1972 vintage) and some 22-year-old is available from a private bottler.

The make is used in Teacher's Highland Cream, a blend with an exceptionally high malt content, and others in the Allied Distillers range.

Of interest nearby

• **Huntly Castle** site has been fortified since the 1100s when a Norman peel was built on land gifted by William the Lion. Robert the Bruce occupied it in the years before Bannockburn. The present ruin dates from the 14th century and the entrance to the round tower has been described as 'the most splendid heraldic doorway in the British Isles'.

Left: The towering ruins of Huntly Castle, also known as the Palace of Strathbogie, retain some remarkable architectural details.

Knockdhu Distillery

Location: **Knock, Banffshire** • *Roads:* **Off the B9022 west of Huntly** **Please telephone for information about visiting** • *Tel:* **01466-771223**

*U*nited Distillers (and forerunners DCL) are one of the biggest distillery owners in Scotland (and, indeed, the world) yet Knockdhu is the only one the company built for itself. The rest were acquired in the 1920s and 1930s as a result of company mergers and distillery owners going out of business in the Depression.

Knockdhu was founded by DCL in 1894 and, like Auchroisk 80 years later, the distillery was built because a spring of particularly good water was found. The owner of the Knock estate had had an analysis made of the water and DCL heard about its quality. They were under contract to supply malt whisky to Haig, the blenders (whom DCL came to own in later years) and needed to buy, or build, a pot-still distillery. Such was the scale of the operation that, when Knockdhu was built on Knock farm, the Great North of Scotland railway company built a station and sidings alongside the distillery specifically to serve it.

The distillery stayed in the same hands until very recently. It had been closed in 1983 but reopened in 1989 under the new owners, Inver House. The whisky is being relaunched under the new name of An Cnoc; it means essentially the same as before but uses the Gaelic spelling and dispenses with 'dhu', which just means 'black'. The core buildings are splendidly solid, made of the local grey granite, and at the outset included a fine house each for the distillery manager and the Excise Officer. Each house had a water-closet lavatory, in those days regarded as a distinct perk and often a matter of animated negotiation by interested parties at the design stage.

3

The whisky is made from spring water, to which the distillery owns the water-rights, from Knock Hill. The tapwater supply to the nearby village of Knock is from the same source. A cooperage was built in 1974. Knockdhu is a small distillery and there has only ever been a single pair of stills in place.

Many distilleries were used to accommodate servicemen during the last war but Knockdhu was lent a more exotic touch than most by the presence there from 1940 to 1945 of a unit from the Indian Army. They even had their own slaughterhouse in the distillery for the halal preparation of their diet.

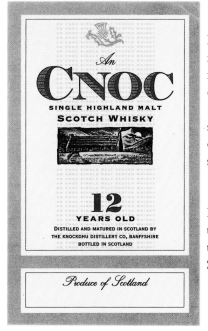

The Whisky

Knockdhu is soft, pleasantly smoky and really rather classy. The flavour is vivid with fruit, malt and lovely spiciness; quite full with an elegant, mellow finish. Officially it has been a 12-year-old at 40% vol. but it remains to be seen what is being planned under the new owners' An Cnoc label. There is presently some 1974 vintage in circulation.

• M o v i n g   o n •

It is a short drive from Knockdhu to the trail's terminus in Keith, where it links directly with the traffic jam of trails that spread out all over Speyside.

Trail 4 🍁 Speyside & Glenlivet

Introduction

Speyside and Glenlivet are two of the most magical and evocative names associated with Scotch whisky. This area is to malts as the Haut Médoc is to claret and Grande Champagne is to Cognac. It is not that all whisky produced here is better than anywhere else; what is striking is that so much of it is consistently excellent and appealing, and that the best emerges as the epitome of elegance, balance and distinction. Distilleries are so thick on the ground in this part of the Highlands that the logical way to look at them is to follow a series of loop-trails centred on the towns around which they cluster: Elgin, Rothes, Dufftown, Aberlour, Keith and Tomintoul. Sites of interest on this trail are listed in association with the towns and not the individual locations.

T r a i l   4 a • Around Elgin

Elgin has been a Royal Burgh since the 1200s and indeed was already a centre of great gentility at that time. The cathedral was burned down by the bad-tempered bastard son of a Scottish king for no reason other than that he had been excommunicated by the Pope of the day. The town's layout, if not many of the actual buildings nowadays, is mediaeval and the little wynds, vennels and pends are picturesque as well as useful shortcuts to those who know their way about.

Above: The ruins of Elgin cathedral are on the outskirts of the town.

Linkwood Distillery

Location: **Elgin, Morayshire** • *Roads:* **On A941 south of Elgin**
Visitors welcome by appointment
Tel: **01343-547004**

This is not only a pretty distillery in an attractive setting; it has facilities to produce spirit in a novel two-unit manner which enabled the Victorian buildings to be retained. The pagoda head is still there, the little dam that is both ornamental and functional lies alongside and the spot is surrounded by mature woodland.

The distillery was built in 1821 by Peter Brown, the factor of the Seafield estates of Moray and Banffshire, and is named after Linkwood House, the family home. Brown's son, William, carried on the business and rebuilt the distillery in the 1870s. Directors of Teaninich and Scapa distilleries were involved at different times in the running of Linkwood. One of the managers in the 1930s believed that absolutely everything in the distillery played its part in making the whisky what it was and he commanded that nothing – not even a cobweb – be removed. Had he lived long enough, he would have been dismayed in 1962 when the internal layout was radically changed and again in 1971 when a second distilling unit with two pairs of stills was built alongside the original Linkwood single-pair set-up.

Glen Grant (*qv*) had also opened another 'branch' across the road at Rothes but found that the spirit produced was so different that the new unit had to be registered as a completely separate distillery and given a different name, Caperdonich. It is perhaps academic now since the old site at Linkwood has been silent since 1985.

The Whisky

Linkwood is light, sweet and gently smoky, but also carries a lovely quiet complexity. There is considerable fruit presence too with a spicy-apple tang. The distillery whisky is 12 years old at 43% vol. but it is a whisky that is particularly cherished by *cognoscenti* and the private bottlers offer a plethora of alternatives. Try the 14-, 15- and 21-year-olds; available vintages go back as far as 1939.

Longmorn Distillery

Location: **Longmorn, by Elgin, Morayshire IV30 3SJ**
Roads: **Off the A941, 4 miles south of Elgin**
Visitors welcome by appointment • No groups
No reception centre or shop • *Tel:* 0154278–3042

———

Longmorn's Victorian persona sits up amid the greenery of the Elgin hinterland, the roof of a great, long warehouse serving as a canvas for the man-sized lettering that announces the distillery name. The site had been a grain mill since the early 1600s.

In 1894, just under 20 years after he opened Glenlossie distillery, John Duff and two partners built Longmorn on the Rothes road south of Elgin that is still today something of a Distillers' Row.

The floor maltings were used until 1970 when they became the distillery boiler-room. Longmorn has four pairs of stills and until recently the four wash stills were coal fired. This was the original direct-flame means of heating stills, a method that took a lot of monitoring and good judgement on the part of the stillman and stoker. One of the reasons this operation was practicable at Longmorn is that the original still house, which had two pairs of stills, was made over to accommodate four wash stills; the neighbouring filling store was then converted to take four corresponding spirit stills. Each building was then able to provide the separate heating arrangements that had been decided upon. The wash stills have rummagers which revolve inside during boiling up to stop solids sticking and burning, and the old waterwheel that can be seen at the distillery was used to power the rummagers in the past. The water for distilling comes from local springs and the peat from mosses on the Mannoch Hill.

The Whisky

The broad characteristics combine fresh, clean nuttiness with a generous, big, velvety mass; usually some smoky richness with sherry background depending on the cask. Longmorn from source is bottled at 15 years and 43% vol. Twelve-year-old and 1956, 1962, 1963 and 1969 vintages are available from independents.

Glenlossie and Mannochmore Distilleries

Location: **Thornshill, Elgin, Morayshire**
Roads: **West of the A941 two miles south of Elgin**
Visitors welcome by appointment • *Tel:* 01343-860331

Glenlossie is one of the more attractive distilleries, with its white-harled buildings clustered beneath the grey slating of the roofs and the ever-watchful pagoda-head of the old kiln. The site is actually a two-distillery complex, the other part being Mannochmore which was built just on 20 years ago.

Glenlossie was built in 1876 by a 'man o' many pairts', as indeed many of the distillers of the time were. John Duff was an innkeeper at Lhanbryde and had also been manager of Glendronach distillery near Huntly. He chose his partners wisely, one being the local public prosecutor and the other the burgh surveyor. The distillery made full use of the Elgin-Perth railway line and had its own siding.

A great fire broke out in 1929 and one of the old fire engines that fought the blaze can still be seen at the distillery. It dates from the 1860s and was designed as a horse-drawn vehicle. The fire held things up for a time but development eventually continued. In 1960 electricity finally arrived to displace steam as the source of power and in 1962 a third pair of stills was added. Apart from their shape, a distinctive aspect of the stills is the purifiers which are fitted to the three spirit vessels. These cylindrical devices help refine the spirit, achieving the opposite effect to that of the Lomond stills used elsewhere to give deeper, heavier distillate.

Above: The distillery has a long history. The barrels being moved to the storeroom back in the 1930s clearly bear the name of Haig.

The Whisky

Quite an elegant style of malt with sweet malt'n'walnut aromas which follow on through the taste. Notably smooth. Glenlossie is a 10 year old malt. Mannochmore make a 12 year old and some vintage 1972 and 1973 currently around. Glenlossie is licensed to the famous Haig firm and is used in most of the Haig blends. It is also one of the half-dozen mainly Speyside malts used to make their vatted malt brand, Glenleven.

Left: Still in full working order, Oldmills Watermill now operates as a museum. The current building dates back to 1793, but there has been a mill on this site for over 750 years.

Of interest around Elgin

• **Elgin Museum**, housed in an Italianate building that is a little unexpected this far north, has wide-ranging collections relating to the locale. In an area of archaeological richness, the displays and interpretations are invaluable.

• **Oldmills Watermill** is the latest in a succession of such working buildings on the same spot going right back to before 1203. It is in full working order producing flour from grain.

• **Moray Motor Museum** has vintage, veteran and classic cars plus oldtime memorabilia.

• The **Doo'cot** at New Elgin goes back 400 years to when lack of feedstuffs made it difficult to sustain livestock through each winter. Having meat to eat meant breeding pigeons and the lairds reserved the right to do so. This beehive-shaped doo'cot was effectively a winter larder for its owner.

Trail 4b • Around Rothes

If you arrived as a visitor to Rothes from the north at the turn of the century, the sight that greeted you would surely have seemed to sum up the Highlands. Immediately before you, at the entrance to the village, not only was there a whisky distillery on each side of the road, but the overhead pipe that ran across the road, like an artery linking a body to some vital source, contained not water, nor fuel, nor milk, but ... whisky.

Rothes is an attractive village in the no-nonsense, slightly austere Highland way and it is best known today for its clutch of five whisky distilleries. In order of appearance, these were Glen Grant, 1840; Glenrothes, 1878; Glen Spey, 1879; Speyburn, 1897; and Caperdonich, 1898. Visiting them in this order is not vital but gives a chance to compare the early buildings and the choice of sites.

The English King Edward I passed south from Elgin through the Glen of Rothes at the head of his invading army in 1296 but the town was not founded until 20

years after Culloden. It was a crofting community and Glen Grant distillery was its first industrial presence. Rothes castle is the flimsy ruin seen today because most of the stonework went clandestinely into building the crofters' cottages.

Left: Rothes Castle shows little of its former splendour.

Glen Grant Distillery

Location: **Rothes, Morayshire AB38 7BS**
Roads: **At north end of village on main road**
Seasons: **Mid March- end October**
Hours: **9.30am - 4pm, Mon - Sat. Sun.12.30-4.00pm**
Groups: **Yes, starting times as required. Explanations in
French, German, Italian, Spanish and Japanese
Reception centre and shop. Admission charges**
Tel: **01542-783318**

Glen Grant opened its doors in Rothes in 1840 and was the first distillery in the town; and for the next 40 years it remained the only one. The distillery was also the first industrial premises in the North of Scotland to have electric light. Glen Grant has played a formative role in introducing malt whisky to consumers outside Scotland, notably in Italy which is now the No 1 world market for malts. The Glen Grant brand is seen as the epitome of malt whisky in Italy where the tradition of drinking it young – say, five years old – is firmly established.

As may be expected, the distillery has some interesting traditions, and there are many anecdotes about early proprietors. Today, VIP guests taken for a short walk in the pretty little glen behind the distillery are usually served a surprise glass of whisky from a bottle stored in a recess by the burn; water is added from a jug filled from the burn. This company tradition goes all the way back to Major James Grant, son of the co-founder of the distillery, whose idea it first was.

Brothers John and James Grant built the distillery at the north end of Rothes in 1840. They had been smugglers and they had also worked Dandaleith distillery near

Above: Distillery workers take a break outside Glen Grant distillery at the end of the 19th century.
Opposite: Hidden in the beautifully landscaped grounds of the Glen Grant distillery is the whisky safe where Major Grant stored bottles to share with friends.

Craigellachie in the 1830s. James qualified as a lawyer and practised in Elgin but he was drawn back to the idea of a distilling partnership with his brother. James was Provost (Mayor) of Elgin for a number of years and he did much to promote the railway throughout the county.

James Grant's son, Major James, built a beautiful mansion nearby as the family home. He also built a second distillery across the road in 1898 called simply Glen Grant No 2 and a famous 'whisky pipe' ran across the road carrying spirit to be merged with the flow on the other side. Glen Grant No 2 closed in 1902 and when revived was designated a separate distillery and named Caperdonich. Once when on safari in Africa, Major James met a young Matabele lad who had become isolated from his family. He brought him back to Rothes, made him his personal valet and, with the similarities to the story of Robinson Crusoe in mind, the locals christened him 'Friday'. He settled down in Rothes and spent the rest of his life in a rent-free flat in the Grant mansion.

The industrial plant just by the distillery on the outskirts of Rothes is unsightly but it should not be regarded too harshly since it represents the combined efforts of otherwise competitor distiller companies to minimise the effects on the area of the effluent they produce. The works transforms the effluent into nourishing cattle feed. The original Glen Grant had floor maltings but, following the inspiration of neighbouring Speyburn, one of the last distilleries to be built in Rothes on a somewhat cramped site, it also installed drum maltings in 1898. The former were closed in 1964 to make way for Caperdonich's renewal, and the latter closed eight years later.

There are four pairs of stills in position now compared to the original two pairs set up with the distillery in 1840. They are coal-fired and, although the new stills – installed in the mid-1980s – are larger than before, they seem to be continuing to produce the same type of spirit. All of the stills have purifiers fitted, which add finesse to the style of the spirit produced.

In the 1980s reconstruction, the worm-tubs were replaced with condensers. The four old stills recently removed had the last rummagers in the Scotch whisky industry to be driven by a waterwheel.

The Whisky

The core flavour of Glen Grant is light, dryish, slightly spirity and gently nutty with sweet, herby overtones. This, however, is developed in many ways by almost endless combinations of age and type of cask used for ageing. There seems to be no definitive Glen Grant at least in terms of age.

The company markets a ten- year-old version, and age-unspecified versions. The independents offer an apparently unlimited choice of ages up to 25 years and over a dozen vintages going back to the mid-1930s.

Speyburn Distillery

Location: **Rothes, Aberlour, Banffshire, AB38 7AG**
Roads: **Off the B9015 north of Rothes**
Please telephone for information about visits
Tel: **01340 831213** *Fax:* **01340-831678**

*T*he setting in which Speyburn sits is absolutely delightful. It is snug on the floor of the vivid green Glen of Rothes and the steepness of the slopes around it contributed to the compactness of its design. The geography meant building upwards instead of outwards and, unusually for country distilleries, most of the buildings, including the warehouses, are on two floors.

Doig was to late-Victorian distilleries as Adam was to neo-classical country houses and the Elgin architect must have relished his working days in this tranquil spot. On a more sinister note, the location was once known as the Gibbet since it was where Rothes criminals were executed. Distillery men may scoff at the idea, but the word is that the night-shift at Speyburn is not too popular...

Speyburn was under construction in 1897 and, since it was Queen Victoria's diamond jubilee, the proprietors were keen to have some whisky distilled within the year for a commemorative edition. They managed to produce some spirit right at the end of December but only by starting distillation before the still house doors and windows had been put in and working in mufflers in the swirl of a snow-storm.

Speyburn was the first pot-still distillery in Scotland to install a drum-malting system, using rotating cylinders filled with barley instead of the old floor-spread method. It went the way of the floor maltings in 1968, however, as owners, United Distillers, continued their policy of using central malting for their distilleries. Speyburn was bought by Inver House Distillers in 1992.

The Whisky

Speyburn is medium-bodied but achieves fair intensity of sweet malt aromas and dryish sappy fruit flavour. Attractive smooth finish. 10 and 21 year old malts are available.

Glenrothes Distillery

Location: **Rothes, Banffshire AB38 7AA** *Roads:* **By the Burn of Rothes**
No reception centre • Please telephone for information about visits.
Tel: **01340-831248** *Fax:* **01340 -831484**

Glenrothes was the town's second distillery after Glen Grant (qv), being completed in 1878 a little way up the glen for which it was named. It was a stormy night in 1879 when the first spirit came off the stills, the gale to the south of the country being strong enough to bring the Tay Bridge crashing down into the river.

Glenrothes was involved in the formation of Highland Distilleries, one of the longest established whisky companies in Scotland. The partnership was first formed in 1887 when W. Grant and Company, owners of Glenrothes, joined forces with the Islay Distillery Company, owners of Bunnahabhain (qv). The distilleries remain in the hands of Highland Distilleries today.

From the time of the creation of the combined company to the early 1960s, very few changes were made to Glenrothes. Then in 1963, the distillery was overhauled and extra still capacity was installed. Glenrothes is a good size and has five pairs of stills, the latest two pairs having been added in 1980.

The Whisky

Glenrothes has a rich, sweet complexity to it from more forward use of oak and peat-reek. It is generous and velvety in texture with good fruit background. The company markets it at 12 years old and 43% vol., while independent bottlings range from eight- to 20-year-olds, and vintages go back to the 1950s.

Glen Spey Distillery

Location: **Rothes, Aberlour, Banffshire AB38 7AY**
Roads: **Off village main street**
Tel: **01340-831215**

*T*he Leslies were the Earls of Rothes and claimed descent from Hungarian nobility. Soldiering Leslies served in the Swedish army, led the Covenanters and stood up as best they could to Cromwell when he gouged his way through Scotland. The ruins of the Leslies' Castle of Rothes still sit on the hill above the town and beneath its slope you will find Glen Spey distillery.

The site is on the Rothes Burn, which is greatly favoured as a source of water – so much so that Glen Spey has to have special gadgets to help condense its spirit. Due to other distilleries further upstream discarding warm water into the flow (which is used only for cooling and never for whisky production), the burn water is not quite cold enough and after-coolers are used in addition to the condensers to convert the still-vapours. On an ecological note, distillers do not discharge hot water directly into burns and rivers, as teeming fish populations indicate; much hot water is now recycled within distilleries or cooled through heat-exchangers before being released back into streams.

James Stuart was a corn merchant with distilling interests in Macallan distillery at Craigellachie in the 1870s. He seems to have built a distilling function on to his oatmeal mill called Mills of Rothes and this expanded to become the fully fledged Glen Spey distillery that he sold to the Gilbey company of London in 1887. This was one of the first moves by a non-Scottish company towards ownership of a Scotch distillery and indicated the extent to which whisky was becoming regarded as an important international product.

The exterior of the distillery is still pleasingly Victorian with solid, weathered stone buildings. Much of the interior, too, is in period. There are two pairs of stills, the second pair being added in 1970 during rebuilding of the distillery. The stills have purifiers fitted to lighten the spirit produced. Water is taken from the Doonie Burn for the production of the distillate itself.

The Whisky

Glen Spey is a light-bodied, elegant malt with floral, exotic aromas and a silky, dry finish.

Of interest around Rothes

Situated just across the road from Glen Grant distillery and originally called Glen Grant No. 2, **Caperdonich** has been registered as a separate distillery for less than 30 years. After being built in 1897 as an additional production unit to the main distillery, it stayed in operation for a mere five years due to the surfeit of whisky in the market at the end of the century and was closed down in 1902. It remained silent for over 60 years before being revived in 1965 with its original stills – their antiquity indicated by the beautifully fashioned riveted seams – always a give-away of old-time distillery equipment. Caperdonich's main role is as a blending whisky.

Left: Restored after 60 years' silence, the Caperdonich distillery is now in use again. Despite using the same malt and water as neighbouring Glen Grant, its whisky is entirely different.

Trail 4c • Around Dufftown

Dufftown began to take shape from 1817 onwards, the idea of the local laird James Duff, the Earl of Fife, who felt that the men who returned from the Napoleonic Wars were entitled to have work. The Town House tower was built in 1836 and is now the Dufftown Museum and information bureau; it used to be the local jail.

The Clock Tower was built in 1839 but the clock itself came from Banff and was the tool of a lynching there in 1700. A known Robin Hood-style bandit called Macpherson, condemned to die there at a specific hour by a legal court, was reprieved in response to a petition from the townsfolk. Knowing that the pardon was on its way, Lord Braco, Sheriff of Banff, had the town clock put forward an hour so that Macpherson could be executed before the document arrived.

Dufftown thrived after the distillery-building Klondyke of the 1890s and someone came up with the idea that, in comparison with Rome which was built on seven hills, Dufftown was built on seven stills. The seven were Mortlach (1823),

Glenfiddich (1887), Balvenie (1892), Convalmore (1894-1985), Parkmore (1894-1931), Dufftown (1896) and Glendullan (1898). The situation has further evolved, however, with Pittyvaich (1975) and Kininvie (1992) having been subsequently added.

Above: Dominating the centre of town, Dufftown Clock Tower is built in a similar style to many of the castles and mansions in this part of the world.

Glenfiddich Distillery

Location: **Dufftown, Keith, Banffshire, AB55 4DH**
Roads: **On the A941, half-mile north of Dufftown**
Seasons: **All year 9.30am - 4.30pm, Mon - Fri except Christmas and
New Year holidays. Also Sat. 9.30am - 4.30pm
and Sun.12.00 - 4.30pm Easter to October**
**Commentaries also in French, German, Italian, Spanish and Japanese
Group bookings over 12 persons by appointment
Reception centre and shop • *Tel:* 01340-820373 *Fax:* 01340-820805**

Glenfiddich were the first to take malt whisky out into the world and, just 30 years after the first steps across the border into England were made in 1963, the familiar triangular bottle has become the top-selling single malt in the world. The Grant family have run the show for five generations and continue to do so today. They are proud of the fact that the entire process of making good whisky may be seen at the distillery. It is the only distillery in the Highlands, and one of only three in Scotland, where the whisky is 'château-bottled' – i.e. bottled where it was made and matured. The stills continue to be coal fired and a noisy, sweltering process you can see it to be from up close. The distillery has its own coppersmiths and coopers.

William Grant worked for 20 years at Mortlach distillery, latterly as manager, and left when he got the opportunity to buy at a bargain price the cast-off stills and other equipment from Cardhu distillery which was being refitted. He completed his own distillery in 1887 and it yielded its first spirit on Christmas Day of the same year. Grant did not have a customer for his first batch of spirit but John Gordon Smith, distiller of The Glenlivet at Minmore, was unable to fulfil an order due to a

4c

*Left: Testing the progress of
maturation in the warehouse.*

fire at his distillery and he
recommended Grant's make to his
customer. The deal went through
and both sides were well satisfied.

To begin with, Grant's three
sons helped him run the distillery
at a time when they were
preparing for entrance to
Aberdeen University; it was not uncommon for visitors to find maths primers and
anatomy books propped up in corners of the distillery to be handy when spare
moments presented themselves. At the same time, Grant's daughters cut the peat for
the kiln. Grant was able to build a second distillery – Balvenie – close by in 1892.

When whisky-blenders Pattison, Glenfiddich's best customer, folded in 1898,
Grant decided to launch his own blend, Standfast. He sent son, Captain Charles, and
son-in-law to Glasgow as salesmen but it took 503 visits to potential clients before
they sold ... a single case. In 1920, Charles Grant bought Glendronach distillery (*qv*)
and it was run by the Grant family until 1960 when it was sold to the Teacher
company. Perhaps if the Grants had held on to Glendronach they would not have
had to build the century's newest distillery, called Kininvie, in 1992. It will be the
21st century before we know how the mature whisky shapes up!

Most of the traditional elements are there to be seen but Glenfiddich is big and
spreads out quite a bit. It has to be since all whisky is matured at the distillery; with
the scale of Glenfiddich's sales, that means warehousing for over 250,000 oak casks
on the premises.

The 11 wash stills and 18 spirit stills are heated by coal-fired direct flame and are
not paired because it is seen as important to the character of the final distillate that
the spirit stills be small in size. Water is drawn from the Robbie Dubh well which is
both plentiful and consistent in its supply. The malt is supplied by external maltsters
to a lightly peated specification.

The Whisky

'Standard' Glenfiddich's lightness and gentleness appeals to first-time malt-drinkers,
while its spare fruit-and-smoke subtlety is liked by more seasoned buffs. The older
editions take on greater softness, girth and sherried complexity with succulent and
well-mellowed balance. The bottling is minimum eight years old at 40/43%, to 30-
year-old in crystal, silver-stopppered decanters. Some 12-year-old has lately been on
offer from one of the independents. Most goes into Grant's own blends.

4c

Glendullan Distillery

Location: **Dufftown, Banffshire, AB55 4DJ**
Roads: **By A941/A920 junction in Dufftown**
All visits by appointment • Reception centre • *Tel:* 01340-820250

Glendullan was a favourite whisky of King Edward VII but it has taken a back seat compared to the other single malts that have been heavily promoted in recent times by its owners. But it was recently chosen by the Speaker of the House of Commons as her special whisky. The site is a pretty spot on the bank of the River Fiddich.

Glendullan was the last of the 1890s surge in building distilleries around Dufftown and, despite the fact that the whisky boom collapsed in the same year that production at Glendullan got under way, the owners managed to stay in business. The only period during which the distillery was silent was in World War II.

Much remodelling took place in 1962 and in 1972 a second distillery was built in the field alongside 'Old' Glendullan to increase capacity. It is self-contained with three pairs of stills. Both units use the same water, 'recipe' and techniques and, despite having stills of different sizes, produce similar spirit. When asked how far apart the two units were, one staff member said that it was just a short distance in good weather, a very long one in bad. The 'old' side was 'mothballed' in 1985.

The old waterwheel was a grand 14 feet (4.3m) in diameter and supplied 16 horsepower to drive the machinery. The 'old' still-house has wooden worm-tubs for converting the vapour to spirit; the new unit uses condensers. Glendullan shared a railway siding with Mortlach next door. The original still house at Glendullan always had just one pair of stills; the second unit has three. The water is drawn from springs in the Conval Hills.

The Whisky

Glendullan is rather big and mouthfilling with zesty sweetness from both oak and sherry presence. The make goes into the blending of the Dewars, Bell's, Johnnie Walker and Old Parr ranges. The malt is not available generally.

Mortlach Distillery

Location: Dufftown, Banffshire AB5 4AQ
Roads: At A941/B9014 junction towards the east of town
Visitors welcome by appointment • Tel: 01340-820318

Mortlach was the first distillery to be built at Dufftown and, until Glenfiddich got going in 1887, it was the only one. It was licensed practically before the ink on the 1823 Excise Act was dry and the distillery built around a well that had been previously well drawn-upon for illicit production. The distillery was a stop-start operation for some time and when J. & J. Grant of Glen Grant bought it they removed the distilling equipment and left it silent. During this time the barley store was used as a place of worship by local members of the Free Church of Scotland until their new church was built in the town. Next, it became a brewery, then finally a distillery again with fine new equipment, and the whisky was given a brand name, 'The Real John Gordon', referring to the owner.

The next proprietor, George Cowie, was a surveyor for the railway companies and later became the provost (mayor) of Dufftown. A distillery employee called William Grant worked at Mortlach for just on 20 years before handing in his notice in 1886. He had decided that he knew enough about distilling by this time to strike out on his own and over the following year he built his own distillery which he called Glenfiddich.

A railway siding linking Mortlach with Dufftown station was created in 1897, electric light went in the following year and a hydraulic lift system was installed in

4c

the warehouses for lifting casks and assorted loads to the upper floors. They have only just been removed. By 1923, Mortlach had developed to the point of becoming almost a complete village. The Cowie family sold out to the owners of Johnnie Walker whisky and Mortlach is still in the hands of successors United Distillers.

A new distillery was built in 1964 but the exterior, including two different kinds of (now decorative) pagoda heads, has retained its look of a turn-of-the-century complex. The floor maltings were used until 1968. The stills at Mortlach are unusual in that they are of different sizes and, although there are three of each type, they are not paired off. In the 1890s three stills were already in place and, in 1897, when capacity was doubled, this meant six individual stills, not three pairs. This has had to be maintained, as to do otherwise would probably have altered the character of the spirit. There is a rather complicated procedure of making different combinations of distillate from each of the stills and using two spirit safes. It is thought to be the reason for the full-bodied character of Mortlach whisky. Worm-tubs are still used to condense the spirit and they are positioned on a large dais outside the still house. New Lauter mashtuns were installed in 1996.

Left: Mortlach was a family business with faithful workers. Old Sandy Collie put in 57 years' work at the distillery.

The Whisky

Mortlach is lightly peated but has extra depth and roundness. The aromas and flavour are smoky, spicy and rich with a dry edge to innate sweetness. The official bottling is at 16 years and 43% vol. but a host of alternatives are available from independents, underlining the regard in which the malt is held. These include stated-age versions of up to 22 years old and intermittent vintages from the 1960s and 1930s.

Dufftown Distillery

Location: Dufftown, Banffshire, AB55 4BR
Roads: In Dullan Glen on the fringe of town
Visitors welcome by appointment • Tel: 01340-820224

*T*his was the sixth distillery to be set up in Dufftown and the fourth in the 1890s. The buildings are authentically 19th century and bunch together beside a stream in an attractive dell surrounded by hills and trees. Dufftown distillery was not custom-built, however, being converted in 1896 from a meal-mill, and yet nothing jars in the apparent homogeneity of the exterior. Most of the adaptation was internal, of course, but the added-on pagoda roof looks as if it might have been in its position from the outset.

The original distillers only lasted a year before selling out to the Mackenzie company that ran Blair Athol distillery (*qv*) at Pitlochry. Arthur Bell & Sons were specialist whisky blenders who bought the Mackenzie company and its two distilleries in 1933.

The floor maltings were used until 1968, after which malt to the distillery's

Above: The future of the Dufftown distillery was assured when Arthur Bell bought it in order to supply the new US market.

specifications was obtained from local suppliers. Now malt is delivered from one of the centralised maltings in the United Distillers group that took over the distillery in 1985. There are three pairs of stills.

The Whisky

Dufftown is light and low-key. It has some flowery elegance and a little bit of biscuity smoke; dry core, sweet edge, quiet but smooth finish. The official version is 15 years at 43% vol. and one of the independents does a 12-year-old. Dufftown is used in Bell's blends, including the brand-leader in the UK.

HIGHLAND
SINGLE MALT *SCOTCH WHISKY*

DUFFTOWN

distillery was established near *Dufftown* at the end of the (19)th The *bright flash* of the KINGFISHER can often be seen over the *DULLAN RIVER*, which flows past the *old stone buildings* of the *distillery* on its way *north* to the *SPEY*. This *single HIGHLAND MALT WHISKY* is typically *SPEYSIDE* in character with a *delicate, fragrant,* almost *flowery* aroma and taste which *lingers* on *the palate*.

AGED **15** YEARS

43% vol   Distilled & Bottled in SCOTLAND DUFFTOWN DISTILLERY, Dufftown, Keith, Banffshire, Scotland   70cl

4c

Balvenie Distillery

Location: **Dufftown, Banffshire**
Roads: **Off the A941 just north of Dufftown**
Not open for visitors

Scottish architect Robert Adam died exactly a century before the construction of Balvenie distillery, yet founder William Grant's love of the second-hand enabled Balvenie to be described today as an Adam distillery. Grant installed stills that had been sold off from other operations in his own two distilleries and he also made abandoned New Balvenie Castle, designed by the Adam brothers in the 18th century and situated on his land, the core of his new distillery.

Balvenie is the sister distillery to Glenfiddich (*qv*) and was built in 1892 just four years after William Grant's first venture on the Fiddich Burn. Grant had obtained inexpensive second-hand distillation equipment to build Glenfiddich and he pursued the same money-saving policy with Balvenie, getting hold of old stills from Glen Albyn and Lagavulin distilleries. Balvenie continues a floor-malting operation, now just about the last on the Scottish mainland. It supplies about 15 per cent of the distillery's malt requirements. Unlike those at Glenfiddich, the four pairs of stills are not coal-fired, but it is waste-heat from next door that creates the steam-heat to boil them. The water source is Robbie Dubh spring, as for Glenfiddich. The peat used is hand-cut locally, dried and seasoned before being used to fuel the malt-kiln.

The Whisky

Balvenie is totally different in character from Glenfiddich, despite its proximity and the fact that both use the same water and peat-reek on the malt. Balvenie is big, sweet, rich and malty – almost an Earl Grey tea mix of oily fruit and astringency. Unctuous, liqueur-like, some oaky tones and sherry form the older Balvenie Classic.

*Left: Balvenie Castle has
commanded the high country above
Dufftown (originally known as
Balvenie) since the 13th century.
The English King Edward I,
Hammer of the Scots, was there
during his raid in 1304, Mary
Queen of Scots visited in 1562,
and the Duke of Cumberland
billeted troops there before Culloden.*

*Left: A stone in Mortlach
Churchyard commemorates
a battle with the Danes.*

Of interest around Dufftown

• **Whisky Smugglers** left a network of trails
that crisscrossed the Grampian foothills. Walker
Geoff Armitage has researched them and leads
treks along their routes, pointing out hides in the
rocks where equipment was stored and pits
where barley was steeped or stored.
Tel: 0340-20892.
• **Mortlach Churchyard** was the scene of a
battle in 1010 in which King Malcolm II saw off
a marauding army of Danes.
• An old **Watch-House**, used to guard the graves against body-snatchers, can be
seen in the graveyard of the same church and the north wall with its postern door
has a leper's squint. (There was a bede-house [refuge] for lepers at nearby Rathven
in the 1200s.)
• **Balvenie Castle** ruins have a double-leaf 'yett' (the Scottish version of a portcullis
gate) that is the only one of its kind in the country. The special feature of a yett was
the way the horizontal bars of the grille pierced the vertical bars and vice versa,
making a defensive gate that was impossible to dismantle other than by melting it – a
sort of architectural knitting in cast iron.
• A New Distillery is now producing spirit in Speyside. The Grants added **Kininvie**
to their Glenfiddich and Balvenie stable in 1992.
• The local **Golf Course** has the highest hole in Britain (over 1,000 feet [305m]).
• The **Clock Tower** has a plaque to George Stephen, co-founder of the Canadian
Pacific Railway, who was born and grew up in George Street in the town.

4
d

Trail 4d • Around Aberlour

I f there was any illicit whisky-making activity at this spot in the early years of the 19th century, the smugglers eventually had to make themselves scarce because in 1812 the local laird located the new village of Charlestown of Aberlour around it. Smooth stones taken from the bed of the Spey were among the building materials used for some of the houses. Aberlour had a famous orphanage, built in 1882 by the Littler family who were local benefactors. The tower next to the high school is all that remains of the buildings.

Distillers, like philanthropists, have the power to see things done in their communities. After a great storm in the 1840s, the town church clock stopped and with it the villagers' timekeeping. Bread was not baked on time, shops opened late, farm-workers lost the early hours and so on. When the Aberlour manager offered a cask of his whisky to anyone who could repair the clock, it was back in service within days.

The village lies on the right bank of the River Spey below the Conval Hills. It is pretty and flower-bedecked in summer, a sometime winner of Scotland in Bloom and Best-Kept Village in Scotland trophies. From Ben Rinnes some claim that on a clear day you can see, not forever, but the smoke from most of the 43 distilleries that surround the mountain. Aberlour shortbread, a famous Scottish butter-cake, is regarded as among the best obtainable.

Above: The river Spey wends its way down from the Cairngorms.

Aberlour Distillery

Location: **Charlestown of Aberlour, AB38 9PJ**
Roads: **On main road of village**
Visitors welcome by appointment, 9am – 11am and 1pm – 4pm
Group bookings, max 25 • No reception centre or shop
Tel: **01340-871204**

*A*berlour distillery was built in 1826, just 14 years after work on the little town itself began. The distillery has thrived although it has burned down twice, on one occasion the entire town population rising from their beds to roll the barrels of whisky out of danger.

Water was initially taken from a well in the grounds used over a thousand years ago for early Christian baptisms by Dunstan, the Pictish saint, who was eventually to become Archbishop of Canterbury. It is now bypassed and spring-water from Ben Rinnes is used.

The distillery, situated at the end of the wide main street, lies on the Lour Burn just 300 metres from where it joins the Spey. There are few vestiges of the Victorian rebuilding but the tree-shaded gate and lodge house at the entrance are attractive. Until recently a sawmill cooperative made use of one of the distillery buildings. There are two pairs of stills dating from 1973.

The Whisky

Aberlour achieves a finely calculated balance between the sweet roundness of sherrywood and the malty delicacy revealed by ex-Bourbon wood. The finish is cream-smooth with zesty, spicy intensity. The standard issue is 10 years old at 40%

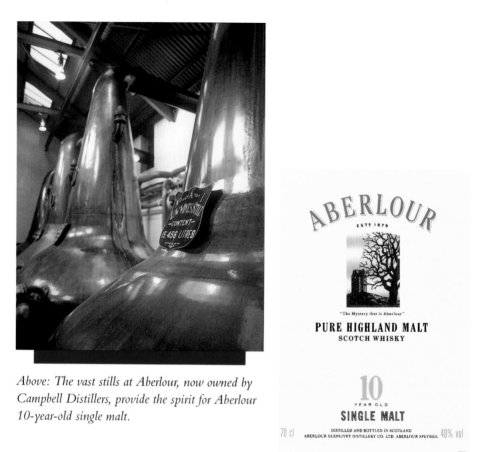

Above: The vast stills at Aberlour, now owned by Campbell Distillers, provide the spirit for Aberlour 10-year-old single malt.

vol. and special editions are regularly offered such as vintages from 1964 (a bottle of which autographed by showbiz celebrities fetched £3,000 at auction), 1969 and 1970 as well as the millenium hogsheads scheduled for release in the year 2000 AD. Wood-type can vary, as with the 1970 which is drawn from a small amount of that year's distillate which was aged exclusively in 30 Bourbon casks. The manager is known to play his bagpipes in the warehouses where the spirit mellows 'just to settle its nerves, ye ken'. Aberlour figures in Clan Campbell blends.

Glenallachie Distillery

Location: **Aberlour, Banffshire** • *Roads:* **Off the A95**
No reception centre or shop • *Tel:* **01340-871315**

Glenallachie is one of the 40-odd distilleries scattered around the countryside below the imposing bulk of Ben Rinnes, the mountain that waters many of them with its countless burns and rivers. The distillery is also one of the latest and its buildings, while neat and tidy, are angular and characterless; as one writer pinpointed it, from a distance you could mistake Glenallachie for a motel. However, the new owners, a subsidiary of French pastis-makers, Pernod, are imaginative and will make the most of the site in terms of both whisky making and presentation to the public.

Over a period of just under 20 years, architect William Delmé-Evans became something of a latter-day Charles Doig in his specialising to a degree in designing distilleries. In 1949 Tullibardine (*qv*) in Perthshire went up, 1960 saw both distillery and style of whisky remodelled at Jura (*qv*) and in 1967 Glenallachie was a wholly new creation that no doubt reaped the benefits of the experience gained by Delme-Evans in the course of the earlier work. Glenallachie was built by the owners of the Mackinlay brands which were subsequently taken over by Invergordon. The latter company 'mothballed' the distillery for a time in the 1980s before Campbell Distillers bought it to add to their distillery stable of Aberlour and Edradour.

The two pairs of stills date from the distillery's construction in 1967, and were designed to produce light, well-textured spirit.

The Whisky

Glenallachie has considerable finesse, with a fragrant delicate persona and appealing botanical freshness. Given its lightness, it is surprisingly round in the mouth. With the distillery's having had three different owners within a short space of time, there may well be some scatter to the official versions in the pipeline but all that seems to be around just now is the 12-year-old at 40% vol. from the Mackinlay days. It is likely to be used in the Clan Campbell blends from now on.

4

Benrinnes Distillery

Location: **Aberlour, Banffshire AB3 9NN**
Roads: **Between the A95 and B9009**
Visitors by appointment only • *Tel:* **01340-871215**

---

*T*he Benrinnes distillery is one of 6 immediately below the Ben that make use of that precious clear water to make their malt whiskies. This is the distillery that was inherited, along with the family estate near Forres, by the young Alexander Edward and which started him in a high-profile career as a whisky promoter and entrepreneur in the years before and after the turn of the century. Benrinnes was not acquired by the Edward family until the 1860s, however, and the first distillery was established in 1826 only to be swept away by the great Speyside floods of 1829. In 1835 a new distillery was built and it was this structure that the Edwards bought from the bankrupt owner in 1864.

A fire brought about rebuilding (including the installation of electric light) in 1896 but Benrinnes remained a combined farm/distillery. A new distillery was built in 1956. A Saladin Box malting system replaced the floor maltings in 1964 and was used for the following 20 years.

Benrinnes is a form of triple-distillation – rare but not unique in Scotland – and the details of the method here produce spirit of around 76% vol., several degrees more than is customarily achieved with double distillation. The stills are grouped in threes, not pairs. There was just one set of stills until 1966 when capacity was doubled to two sets – i.e. six stills.

Benrinnes offers the opportunity to see worm-tubs, the traditional pipe-spirals immersed in cold water, to condense the vapours produced by the stills. The Scurran and Rowantree burns are snow-melt (or snow-bree, as they say locally) which runs down that hard-stone face of Ben Rinnes and makes itself available for the production of the whisky that bears the name of its source.

The Whisky

Benrinnes is made from lightly peated malt. It is sweet and fruity with a spicy unctuousness that gives it the qualities of a light liqueur. There is a touch of smoke and nuts throughout which finishes with quiet intensity. It is bottled by the proprietors at 15 years old and independent versions go up to 18 years old with a 1969 vintage still in circulation.

Left: The mountain of Ben Rinnes gives its name to a type of granite which is extremely slow to erode, making the water that runs off it almost wholly pristine.

Glenfarclas Distillery

Location: **Ballindalloch, Speyside AB37 9BD**
Roads: **Off A95 between Aberlour and Grantown-on-Spey**
Seasons: **April – September, 8.30am – 5.00pm, Mon – Fri;**
also June – September, Sat, 10am – 4pm; October – March, 10am –
4pm, Mon – Fri • Tours until one hour before stated closing times •
Group bookings by appointment. • Reception centre and shop
Tel: **01807-500257** *Fax:* **01807-500234**

Glenfarclas is one of the supreme Scotch whiskies, the Speyside malt that attracted a lot of attention when someone at a tasting described it as 'going down singing hymns'. The distillery is still an independent family-run business, there having been five generations of the Grants and all of the males called either John or George. The slopes of Ben Rinnes rise from behind the distillery grounds and in the spring fingers of snowmelt begin to rush downwards; one such runs through the main yard at Glenfarclas.

Over the years the Grant family have had one or two points of contact with the Royal Family who traditionally spend part of the late summer in this part of the Highlands. The grandfather of the present managing director of the distillery, John Grant, was invited to Balmoral in his time to shoot with King George V, but John Grant's own Royal contact was a little more painful. During a schooldays game of cricket at Gordonstoun a ball driven by the other side struck him full in the face. The batsman was Prince Charles.

A tenant-farmer called Hay built the distillery in 1836 and the Grants bought it in 1865 when Hay died. John Grant did not himself work the distillery to begin

Left: The visitors' centre at Glenfarclas is topped with its own pagoda head, and the details of the building have an oriental simplicity.

with, however, letting it out for five years to John Smith who then went off to build Cragganmore at Ballindalloch. Grant began distilling in 1870. The Grants, more than most in the Scotch whisky world at the time, were directly affected by the bankruptcy of the Pattison firm in 1898 – the Edinburgh blenders were the Grants' partners in Glenfarclas! To make matters worse, the distillery had just been rebuilt and there were costs to recoup. By a supreme effort, all creditors were paid and the distillery was secured once again in the family name and the situation has never changed since. The whisky is very highly thought of within the trade and indeed one soliloquy of praise used in promotional literature for Glenfarclas is a direct quote from rival distiller, Tom Dewar, founder of the Dewar's White Label brand.

A businessman visiting Glenfarclas recently was assailed with an overwhelming sense of *déja vu* when he walked into the visitor centre after his tour of the distillery. Mystified, he eventually focused on the elegant oak panelling around the walls and when he was told that it had been salvaged from the old passenger liner, the SS Empress of Australia, he realised that he had once travelled to North Africa on board the ship when the panelling was in its original position.

A bonus for visitors at Glenfarclas is being admitted to the store where the whisky casks are filled. It was opened not long ago by Ian McCaskill, the popular BBC weatherman, who ceremonially filled the first cask. 'As you can see,' he told those present, 'the puppet on the TV *Spitting Image* show is actually better looking than the original.' The floor maltings closed in 1972 and medium-peated malt is brought in from professional maltsters. The distillery's location is quite exposed and in winter arrangements are made to be self-sufficient in everything needed for whisky making for up to a month – just in case the snowdrifts lie longer and deeper than usual.

Three pairs of larger-than-average stills, all of them over 20 years old, are fired by an external gas flame; quite rare these days.

In bygone days, the Ballindalloch Grants used to fall out regularly with the Carron Grants next door. What is now Glenfarclas was on the front line and it is still possible to discern the no man's land strip running up the flank of Ben Rinnes at the edge of the distillery's property. Realising the unclaimed status of the narrow ribbon of land, some canny crofters built cottages on it and moved in. No landlord, no rent!

During the summer months, vintage car rallies make the distillery one of the check-in points.

The Whisky

Glenfarclas is rich and round, sherried, concentrated and zesty. Smoke and vanilla from the oak flash through here and there and the whole is immensely well mellowed. It is issued in a wide range of editions by the proprietors themselves giving a spectrum of how the whisky develops from 10 to 25 years old. The '105' is cask strength, 60% vol., and claimed to be the strongest whisky on the market. This is how Scotch malt used to be drunk – straight from the cask.

Glenfarclas used to be produced in conventional and 'clear' versions, the former with a sherrywood emphasis, the latter from Bourbon wood only. Now all Glenfarclas spirit is aged in at least 80 % sherrywood at the distillery and, so that it may be a wholly consistent style, none is released for private bottling as a self whisky. Some slip through the net, however, and an 11-year-old was recently available from one of the independents. One experiment that was kept strictly in-house was the Glenfarclas aged in a port pipe. Delicious, reported John Grant, but it could not really be described as Scotch whisky. Glenfarclas is widely used for blending but the brand names are confidential.

Cragganmore Distillery

Location: **Ballindalloch, Banffshire AB37 9AB**
Roads: **Off the B9137 near Bridge of Avon**
Visits by appointment
Reception centre • *Tel:* 01807-500202

---

*B*allindalloch is the inland terminus of the northern section of the Speyside Way, the walkway that follows the line of the old railway track that ran along the side of the beautiful River Spey. The distillery buildings lie in a hollow in the lee of Craggan Mor Hill around their own stretch of fast-flowing burn, which empties into the Spey just below.

This is classic Highland malt whisky country – meadows, woodland, outcrops of hard rock and fast water. Nearby is Ballindalloch Castle, a fine house in the Scottish Baronial style and home of the Macpherson-Grants. The family have long taken a special interest in the distillery and they lay down casks of Cragganmore for their own use. They do not stand on ceremony; when stocks run low at the castle, a caller simply turns up at the distillery, pays the Excise duty, puts a cask in the back of the Range Rover and drives off.

Cragganmore founder, John Smith, wholeheartedly embraced the facility of the railway and travelled everywhere by train. However, because of his great 22-stone girth, he was unable to squeeze through the carriage doors and always had to travel in the guard's van. The leather armchair he had made to measure for himself is still at Cragganmore. The distillery was the first to plan its layout and distribution to suit the new rail transport and in 1887, a year after John Smith died, the first 'Whisky

d

Special' train steamed out of Ballindalloch station with a load of 16,000 gallons. The event is recorded on the label of the 12-year-old.

Smith was one of the foremost distillers of his time. He had already managed the distilleries of Macallan, Glenfarclas and Glenlivet (of whose founder he is thought to have been an illegitimate son) when in 1869 he obtained a lease from Sir George Macpherson-Grant to set up his own operation at Ayeon Farm on the Ballindalloch Estate. Cragganmore was the first new pot-still distillery in the area since the 1840s and Smith wanted to tap into the 1860s whisky boom. After his death his son, Gordon, took over and in 1901, a time when distilleries were closing down everywhere, he brought in Charles Doig to rebuild the distillery. The fact that he

could even contemplate such expenditure underlines the extent to which Cragganmore was a first-choice malt on the market.

For a long time Cragganmore was a mixture of ancient and modern – electric light was installed in 1919 but new buckets were being ordered for the waterwheel as late as 1950, a year before national grid electricity became accessible.

The public side-road ends at Cragganmore and there is still something of the feel of the old self-contained Highland distilling communities about the place. Family houses line the fringe of the distillery grounds; the visitors' reception area, known as the Cragganmore club resembles a Victorian Gentleman's sporting club. It is finished like a drawing room; they have their own snow-ploughs to clear the roads in winter and get the children out to school; and most of the men can turn their hand to a wide range of skills.

Cragganmore's two pairs of stills are unusual in that the lyne-arms at the top, which rise like swan-necks in other distilleries, taper horizontally in a T-shaped configuration. John Smith designed them this way so they probably have much to do with Cragganmore's aristocratic fine spirit. Worm-tubs for condensing the spirit are still used.

d

Above and right: Some of the 'family' of employees at work, checking the washback and the stills during the whisky-making process.

The Whisky

Cragganmore is a very fine, aristocratic malt with excellent malt and smoke details. Drier than many Speysides, it has complexity and length, but delivers quietly. Only recently widely available as a self whisky, it is 12 years old at 40% vol. but 20-year-old and some vintages from the 1970s are available from other bottlers.

The malt is used in blends under the Macallum brand which quirkily markets Scots, not Scotch, whisky and is popular in Australia and New Zealand.

Tormore Distillery

Location: **Advie, Grantown-on-Spey, Morayshire PH26 3LR**
Roads: **On A95 between Grantown and Bridge of Avon**
Visits by appointment only • No reception centre or shop
Tel: **01807-510244**

*A*s you turn a bend on the A95 on Speyside Tormore suddenly looms large before you. It is solidly built in light-coloured granite but the details – great arched windows, stone balustrading, fine strip-fenestration on the roof-ridge – lend the distillery considerable style and originality. When it was completed in 1960, the first new distillery in Scotland this century, it created a whole new community with its clutch of pretty tied cottages laid out behind.

The architect was Sir Albert Richardson, a past president of the Royal Academy, who succeeded in creating a main building that was different from the classic Highland distillery but which equally avoided the visual curse of the concrete and glass boxes to which remodelled distilleries were starting to be reduced. Sir Albert included a small curling pond in the layout and he tried to mask the mandatory tall chimney by rendering it as a giant whisky bottle, but there were problems in constructing it and the idea was abandoned.

There are four pairs of stills, each with a purifier to lighten the spirit. The malt used to make Tormore is lightly peated and the whisky is matured principally in ex-Bourbon casks.

A time-capsule in the shape of a pot-still was buried in the forecourt of the distillery, the intention being to open it in the year 2060. It contains assorted data about whisky and Scotland for future industrial archaeologists including a history of

Above: Even in a modern distillery, time-honoured methods of testing the water have to be followed.

the clans, the names of the Tormore staff in 1960 and samples of barley, local water, peat and cask staves. The excavators should have some glasses handy too since there is a tregnum of Long John, the owners' blended whisky brand, for them to sample.

The Whisky

Tormore has finesse and a certain, straight nobility to its personality. It is subtle,

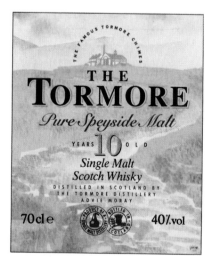

nutty and has a light, but velvety, texture. It understates all the way yet stays on well at the end. Long John bottle it at 10 years and 40/43% vol. and independent versions are scarce. Not surprisingly Tormore is used in the Long John Blends.

Knockando Distillery

Location: **Knockando, Morayshire**
Roads: **Off the B9102** • *Tel:* **01340-810205**

*T*his is the distillery that supplies much of the malt content of J & B blended whisky, one of the world's biggest-selling brands. It sits on a high wooded bank of the Spey and, viewed from the opposite side of the river, the pagoda-head, shoulders and whitewashed flanks rise splendidly from the dense tree-foliage that clusters closely around them. The parish was the home of the Grant brothers upon whom Charles Dickens based his Cheeryble brothers in Nicholas Nickleby.

Knockando distillery was built in 1898 just as the whisky crash was looming and the original owners had to sell out very soon afterwards. Gilbey's, forerunners of IDV who now own it, acquired the business in 1904 so Knockando has been in the same hands for most of its existence. When the old malt barns went out of use, assorted local events took place in them. One such was a flower show in the 1930s, which was opened by the British Prime Minister, Ramsay Macdonald; when the company won the Queen's Award for Export Achievement in 1985, another premier, Margaret Thatcher, was on hand at the distillery to receive the billionth bottle of J & B Rare to be produced.

The floor maltings were discontinued in 1968 and turned over to warehouse space. The owners now take lightly peated malt from local maltsters. There are two pairs of stills.

Knockando distillate intended for blending ages at any distillery in the group

where there is room to store it. Distillate for bottling as a self whisky, however, is always warehoused at the distillery, a certain proportion in sherrywood.

Above: The main office at Knockando still has a Victorian charm.

The Whisky

Knockando is light and elegant with wreathing garden aromas and smooth, soft, nutty flavours. All bottled Knockando single malt is vintage in the sense that the year of distillation is stated on the label. The idea is to market the whisky when it is ready, rather than at a specific age, so the vintages are usually from 12 to 15 years old when they first go on sale.

Knockando figures prominently in J & B blends from the 'standard' Rare right up to the older de luxes. J & B make a thing of the light colour of their whiskies, preferring not to add the caramel used cosmetically by other firms. Knockando spirit is no longer sold outside the group's sister companies so alternative ages and strengths from independents are now few and far between.

Tamdhu Distillery

Location: **Knockando, Morayshire IV35 7RR**
Roads: **On the B9102 between Archiestown and Knockando**
Not open to visitors

*T*amdhu has a couple of unique nuggets of originality that make it a particularly pleasing visit. It is the sole remaining distillery in Scotland with Saladin Box maltings which are still in use, and the reception centre is the former Victorian railway station of Knockando.

Tamdhu was built in 1896 by a consortium of whisky blenders but it was sold on just three years later to Highland Distilleries who have owned it ever since. Tamdhu was silent from 1927 until 1947 before going on to be expanded and rebuilt in the 1970s. The distillery has buildings from several different periods.

The floor maltings were replaced with a Saladin Box system in 1951 which continues to supply the entire malt requirement of the distillery. The germinating barley is shifted by mechanical turners which travel back and forth at regular intervals along the 10 shallow troughs in which it is lies. Air is blown through holes in the trough-floors to control the temperature of the barley.

The drying kiln is modern with hot air blown through the malt, cutting the customary time of the operation by half. This air is pre-heated by waste hot water coming from the condensers on the stills. Locally collected peat is burned in a small furnace and the smoke intermingled with the drying air in the kiln to add the degree of smokiness appropriate to Tamdhu spirit. There was a single pair of stills until 1972 when a second pair was added. In 1975 the distillery was largely rebuilt, including the installation of a third pair of stills. The distillery is located around a spring which furnishes the production water.

Left: Tamdhu distillery is set in dense woodlands. The old railway station became the visitor centre, which is now closed.

The Whisky

Tamdhu is light, smoky and well balanced, developing a ripeness of biscuity flavour that is surprisingly lengthy. Some toasty sweetness and tiny spice. The whisky is now marketed as a "no age statement" single malt. It is used in the make-up of the Famous Grouse blend.

Cardhu Distillery

Location: **Knockando, Aberlour, Banffshire AB38 7RY.** *Roads:* **On B9102**
Seasons: All year, 9.30am - 4.30pm, Mon - Fri;
also Easter - September, Sat as above
July - September: Sun 11.00am - 4.00pm
Group bookings by appointment
Reception centre, shop, exhibition, coffee shop, picnic area
Tel: **01340-810498 •** *Fax:* **01340-810491**

*W*hen John Cumming first licensed his Cardhu distillery in 1824, he had a string of convictions as a whisky smuggler behind him. Such brushes with the law seem to have been the equivalent then of parking on a double yellow line today. They even became a kind of alternative pedigree and at Cardhu the court judgements are framed and hung proudly on the wall of the distillery manager's office.

Cumming took a lease at Cardhu farm in 1811 and made whisky from the outset. He was a classic example of the tenant-farmer for whom distilling was a related part-time farming activity using barley, peat and water from the land to good productive ends. His wife, Helen, was an inspired partner. She looked after the mashing and fermenting and always succeeded in disguising it as bread-making if the Excise officers happened by. She would sit them down for tea and bannocks and, while they ate, would slip out and fly a red flag from the barn – a prearranged signal to her neighbours to hide their distilling equipment since there were revenue men in the area. She lived to the age of 95, still involved with whisky, and is remembered selling it at a shilling a bottle through the kitchen window at Cardhu farm. Even

Left: At work in the filling-store attached to Cardhu.

after being licensed, Cardhu's whisky was produced on this simple artisanal basis because Cumming liked the status of being one of the smallest distilleries in Scotland but also one of the best. His son and daughter-in-law, Elizabeth, kept faith with his approach even after he died, but finally, in 1884, the worn-out equipment was replaced by the new Cardhu distillery. It was situated on additional land leased in perpetuity by Elizabeth, now a widow, who was a talented, dynamic woman and probably the most accomplished woman distiller of her time. Among the plant she sold off were a pair of much-patched and very thin-skinned pot-stills that went to a new distiller called Mr. Grant for £120. He was optimistic that he could do well with the whisky he was going to produce and his distillery was to be called Glenfiddich.

By the 1890s, Cardhu had become the principal malt in the blends produced by John Walker & Co., Kilmarnock. In 1893 Cardu was sold to Walker's thus securing supplies for the blends which have become the biggest selling brands in the world with Cardhu remaining the 'heart' of the blend.

The Mannoch Hill nearby provided both the spring water and the peat with which Cardhu whisky was made. In the days when it was illicitly produced, small kegs of it were carried on ponies, often at night, over the Mannoch Hill and down into Forres and Elgin where there was never any shortage of customers.

In the 1920s, the distillery workers' cottages had running water, indoor toilets and electric light long before such amenities were widespread in the countryside. A cask of hot water was placed outside the boiler room every morning from which families drew amounts as required. Elizabeth Cumming's son, John, ran the distillery for Walker's and, for a time, he and the local laird owned the only two motor cars to be seen in the village.

Today the office, the malt-barns and the kiln, including pagoda heads, remain of Elizabeth Cumming's 'New' Cardhu of 1884; the rest of the distillery dates from major refurbishment carried out in 1960. In the 1920s experiments with a form of steam-heating of the stills took place but it was found to be too expensive and discontinued. The technology was better, of course, half a century later and in 1971 Cardhu's three pairs of stills were converted to heating by internal steam coils.

The Whisky

Cardhu is a highly approachable malt – smooth, sweet, mellow and uncomplicated. It has good body and length. It is widely available at 12 years old and 40% vol. with no special editions or older versions, either from the proprietors or the independents.

Imperial Distillery

Location: **Carron, Morayshire AB38 7QP**
Roads: **Off the A95 and B9102**
Please telephone for information about visits
No reception centre • *Tel:* 01340-810276

*I*mperial was built in 1897 and so named in rather oblique tribute to Queen Victoria whose Diamond Jubilee fell on the same year. The malting kiln of the original construction was topped out with an enormous gilt imperial crown. It lasted until the 1955 refit of the distillery when, with its golden colour having given way to that of rust, it was taken down. Thomas Mackenzie set up the venture to keep up with the 1890s' demand for whisky. No one could have been expected to foresee the 1899 collapse of the whisky market, and Imperial closed within just two years of its opening.

World War I came and went before it opened again and this time it lasted six years before closing in 1925 and passing to new owners. It was 1955 before production began again, this time with completely rebuilt equipment. Imperial was silent yet again in the 1980s but it changed hands in 1989 and is now operational.

Stone-built constructions have traditionally held sway in Scotland, but in planning Imperial, Charles Doig decided to use red Aberdeen bricks for the external skin of the buildings.

At around 36,000 litres' capacity, the original stills were very large; compare this with the 11,000-litre wash still and the 3,600-litre spirit stills at Macallan. A forest of belts and pulleys was driven by a turbine and when it broke down a farm tractor had to be backed into position to get things going again.

It was at Imperial that research was carried out into converting the waste material from distillation into nourishing cattle feed.

The Whisky

Another of the rich, simmering, smoky malts that Speyside offers intermittently. It is not pungent or aggressive, but rather soft and gracious with a slight perfumed flavour. No official self whisky from Imperial was bottled but the occasional vintage, such as recently 1979, becomes available from independents.

Dailuaine Distillery

Location: **Carron, Morayshire**
Roads: **Off the A95 one mile south of Aberlour • No reception centre**
Please telephone for information about visits • *Tel:* 01340 810361

---

*T*he Dailuaine distillery was established in 1851 by a farmer called Mackenzie. It sat in a hollow with river meadows all around so he called it Dail Uaine, 'green valley' in the Gaelic. When Mackenzie died in 1865 his widow, Jane, joined the ranks of early Scottish women distillers but she also leased the distillery out to an Aberlour banker for a while. When the Dailuaine-Talisker Distilleries Ltd. company was formed in 1898, Carron's other distillery, Imperial, became part of the little group.

Much of the 1884 rebuilding disappeared in a fire in 1917 but the red Victorian postbox set into the warehouse wall just outside the distillery (and still in use) shows that some fragments remain. Steam and water powered operations into the 1960s although there was electric light from the 1920s onwards. In 1960 the floor maltings were converted to a Saladin Box system which, although not used since 1983, is still in situ. Dailuaine whisky is lightly peated. The original stills were a three-unit system of one large wash still and two small spirit stills. By the 1950s this had changed to a two-pair set-up and in 1960 a further pair was added, making three large double-sets in all.

The distillery had its own 'pug' steam locomotive, bought just before World War II and which was only relinquished because the dreaded Dr. Beeching of British Railways axed the Strathspey line in 1967. Happily part of the line has been revived by enthusiasts and the much-loved pug is now part of the locomotive stock at Aviemore.

The 100-acre farm at Carron Mains, first leased by the Mackenzie family, is still attached to the distillery and produces beef-cattle and grain.

The Whisky

Quite a distinctive malt with a lot of facets crowding together – spice, pepper, sweetness, malt and smoke. It is marketed at 16 years and 43% vol. but there are even more senior versions – 1971, 1972, 23- and 27-year-old – on offer from independents. Dailuaine is one of the malts in the Johnnie Walker range of blends.

Macallan Distillery

Location: **Craigellachie, Banffshire**
Roads: **Near B9102 turn-off to Archiestown**
Visitors to Elchies House welcome by appointment • *Tel:* 01340-871471

Macallan is one of the great malt whiskies of Scotland, its reputation for finesse, richness and complexity at least partly due to the exclusive use of sherrywood for ageing its whisky. Hardly any sherry is shipped to the UK in cask anymore, and Macallan were the first distillers to take special steps to meet their needs. New oak casks are commissioned in Jerez, Spain, and used for ageing sherry for two or more years before being shipped as whole barrels to Scotland to host Macallan spirit. Only 30 years ago Macallan was essentially a local whisky and was not advertised. The company's first annual promotion budget for the bottled malt amounted to £25 for a poster for a sponsored shinty match; today its advertising costs run into millions of pounds worldwide.

The distillery was sold to Highland Distillers and Suntory of Japan in 1996, having been partly owned by the same family for a century.

There are two still houses and 21 stills, and since each wash still supplies two spirit stills instead of the customary one, Macallan has trios, not pairs, of stills.

The Whisky

Macallan is particularly praised for its rich and profound flavours. The sherrywood certainly endows much of the succulence but it is worth noting that 'new' Macallan direct from the still is considered to be a complex, fine and balanced malt. There are a number of official releases between 10 and 25 years old, with seven-year-old specifically for the Italian market where malts are drunk young. With such a range there is less scope for the independents other than for batches that might crop up from time to time with different cask treatment.

4
d

Craigellachie Distillery

Location: **Craigellachie, Aberlour, Banffshire**
Roads: **On hill to the south of the village**
Tel: **01340-881212**

Craigellachie village makes the very best of a spectacular site, terracing its cottages into a hill that looks on to the meeting of the Rivers Spey and Fiddich. Telford's little Meccano bridge of granite and cast iron across the Spey itself dates from 1814. The sign-writing on the modern distillery of Craigellachie declares clearly its associations with White Horse blended whisky and indeed the originator of the brand, the dynamic Peter Mackie, was one of its first partners when the distillery opened in 1891.

Apart from Peter Mackie, the other main mover in setting up Craigellachie was estate-owner Alexander Edward who was a well-known distillery promoter and entrepreneur at the time. He had inherited Benrinnes distillery from his father and became involved in running many distilleries like Dallas Dhu, Aultmore and others. He also leased out his own estate land near Forres for distillery ventures such as Benromach. Edward withdrew from the partnership in Craigellachie in 1900 and by 1915 Mackie had control of the business.

The original distillery was another of those designed by Charles Doig of Elgin but most of his structure was razed in the rebuilding of 1964/65. All that remains of his work are part of a warehouse and the original floor maltings, including the kiln and its external pagoda-head roof. Ironically, some primitive accommodation

d

bothies (shelters), already *in situ* before the distillery was built and used for a long time as temporary storage shelters, are still standing. There used to be a hamlet of 17 distillery houses nearby and in the 1920s the company gave annual prizes for the best-kept gardens. There are two pairs of stills, the second pair dating from 1965.

The Whisky

Craigellachie has an interesting combination of smoky pungency and lightish body. Some fruit and sweetness also show through. 14 year-old Craigellachie Malt is now bottled by United Distillers as a single malt and is sold at the distillery. Predictably the malt is used in the White Horse blends.

Above: Even back in the roaring twenties, White Horse Whisky had its distinctive logo, seen here on the side of a 'horseless cart'.
Left: Barrel lids stacked up outside one of the Victorian cottages built to house workers at Craigellachie.

4
d

Of interest around Aberlour

• **Aberlour Visitor Centre** has nutshell presentation of the history and heritage of the village and its environs.

• **Ballindalloch Castle** is the 16th-century seat of the Macpherson-Grants, local lairds on whose land many of the distilleries in the district first got going. The house represents a transition-point in Scottish fortified houses between the stark keep built for protection and the more comfortable but still secure country house. The gardens

Above: The River Spey meanders across the valley at Craigellachie. Some of the distilleries in this area are on raised sites, overlooking the river, and often tucked away in quieter valleys.
Left: The river is renowned for its salmon fishing.

Above: Ballindalloch Castle, dating back over 400 years, has a freshly scrubbed look that sets it apart from some of the smoke-blackened buildings of the distilleries.

are lovely, with both the Spey and the Avon flowing through the grounds. There is a touch of Disney in the old bridge and gatehouse peeking out from the trees.

• **Speyside Cooperage Visitor Centre** at Craigellachie is attached to a large working cooperage and has a viewing gallery from which visitors may watch the coopers at work. Find out everything about coopering from the acorn to the completed cask.

• The **Malt Whisky Trail** is a signposted route around eight distilleries in the Moray District and it also takes in the cooperage.

• **Speyside Way Visitor Centre** at Boat of Fiddich has complete access to information regarding the long-distance walkway that follows the line of the River Spey and thus passes the doors of a number of distilleries. A good alternative way to visit some of them.

• The **Village Store** in Aberlour has clothing, household effects and utensils from the early part of the century on display. A combination of nostalgia and curiosity builds up during visits.

*e*4

Trail 4e • Around Keith

Keith is the hub of the surrounding farmland with agriculture, as well as woollens and whisky, as a mainstay of the local economy. Latterday Keith, like so many other Highland towns, was a planned community but there was already a settlement here in 700 AD and in 1195 Keith was included in a charter of lands granted by William the Lion to the Abbey of Kinloss. Burgh status was conferred by Charles II but the town today is based on the town planning set in train by the local laird in 1750. This was in the wake of the last Jacobite Rebellion and the bloody nose the Highlanders handed out to the Duke of Cumberland's army at Keith may have been one of the reasons for his murderous behaviour at Culloden.

Milton Tower is all that is left of a larger castle that dates from 1480 and which belonged to the Ogilvies, local lairds at the time. The family went on to acquire its very own saint, John Ogilvie, who was martyred in 1615 and is Scotland's first post-reformation saint.

Above: The packhorse bridge at Keith used to be the only river crossing in town.

Glen Keith Distillery

Location: **Station Road, Keith, Banffshire**
Roads: **Just off the A96 by railway station in Keith**
Visitors welcome by appointment • No groups
No reception centre or shop • *Tel:* **01542-783044**

Glen Keith distillery is a recent operation in historical terms, being a meal-mill converted in 1958 to its present distilling function. It was the first new malt-distilling operation mounted (if not the first distillery actually built) in Scotland since the Apache-charge of construction in the 1890s and there were other innovations later on. The country's first gas-fired still was set up in 1970 and the first microprocessor for controlling aspects of production was installed 10 years later. The distillery lies on a bank of the River Isla just across from its delightful sister distillery, Strathisla (qv).

Chivas Brothers made an excellent job of sympathetically converting the old grain mill, much of whose original fabric had already been demolished before they took it over. They even put a token pagoda-head atop a tower but, since kilns tended not to have windows, it does look a little like a Daliesque campanile. Glen Keith looks the more compact for its not having any warehouses and spirit is taken to company warehouses just outside the town. The distillery has an intact Saladin Box malting system, though it has not been used since 1976.

Glen Keith started with a set of three stills in order to triple-distil its spirit. This was because very light, smooth and understated distillate was wanted for blending. This was discontinued in 1970 when two more stills were added and the distillery went over to double-distillation, leaving one of the stills silent. In 1983 a sixth was added.

The Whisky

Glen Keith is soft, delicate and gently fruity. Some distant peat and toffee; quite round in texture, understated overall. Glen Keith, now bottled in its own right, is the heart of Passport Scotch, one of the fastest growing brands in the world.

Strathmill Distillery

Location: Keith, Banffshire
Roads: Turn off the A96 by the Union Bridge • *Tel:* 01542-882295

During the whisky boom of the 1880s and 1890s, distillers looking to expand production and entrepreneurs trying to get some of the action snapped up disused and derelict mills of all sorts for conversion into distilleries.

Strathmill distillery in its original form was a flour and corn mill that had operated on its site since early in the century. Coincidentally it was constructed in 1823 when the freedoms of the new Excise Act set in motion an earlier distillery-building boom. According to a batch of contemporary local newspapers that were embedded with the foundation stone of the whisky-making installations, there had also been a distillery on the spot in the 1820s. It was probably part of the mill operation, added in the wake of the 1823 Act.

Seen from the banks of the stream, the twin pagoda roofs of the kilns and the zigzag lines of the warehouse gables are delightfully evocative of their era. The cornmill's whisky-making role was established in 1891 and the distillery called Glenisla-Glenlivet. It was the done thing at the time for distilleries to attract a little more attention to their product by hyphenating the celebrated but already-protected Glenlivet name with their own. Just four years later Glenisla was sold to W. & A. Gilbey of London, who changed the name to Strathmill.

There are two pairs of stills, the second pair dating from 1968. The spirit stills have purifiers on the lyne-arms to lighten the spirit. The River Isla only supplies the water for cooling; the water to make the whisky comes from a spring in the grounds.

The Whisky

Strathmill is light, gently fragrant of malt and keen fruit, and finishes smoothly with only slightly peaty zest. It was previously obtainable as a self whisky but all the make now goes to blending, particularly for the J & B and Dunhill ranges.

Strathisla Distillery

Location: **Keith, Banffshire AB55 3BS**
Roads: **Seafield Avenue, sign-posted off the A95**
Seasons: **End Jan to Mid Dec** *Hours:* **9.30am - 4pm, Mon - Sat**
Sun 12.30 - 4.00pm
Group bookings, max 50; starting times as required
Reception centre and shop. Admission charges
Tel: **01542-783044**

*T*his is not only possibly the oldest distillery in Scotland; it is also a candidate for the cutest little distillery in the world. It sits there like a Hansel-and-Gretel cottage with enormous twin pagoda heads over low walls, a waterwheel and a bumpy little lawn and you cannot help smiling at its outrageous appeal.

When the distillery was built Robert Burns was becoming famous and fashionable

Left: The spirit safe at Strathisla proudly announces when the distillery was established.

with the publication of his *Poems Chiefly in the Scottish Dialect*, Goethe began his Italian journey and Mozart's *Marriage of Figaro* was performed for the first time.

Strathisla began in 1786 as Milltown distillery and had a succession of licensees until 1830 when William Longmore began 38 years of ownership. He had to rebuild substantially after a fire in 1876 and it was then that the distillery took on the appearance that we see today. It was also in the 1870s that the name was first changed to Strathisla. Much later, George Pomeroy, a London financier who owned the distillery until 1949, was jailed for tax evasion and the following year Seagram bought it through its subsidiary, Chivas Brothers.

The water with which Strathisla is made is drawn from the Fons Buliens, a spring that was documented by Dominican monks who lived nearby in the 12th century. There are two pairs of steam heated stills.

The Whisky

Strathisla begins placidly but fills out to quite mouth-filling proportions. Very fruity, sweet and herby with fine succulent zest and creamy, peaty intensity. The official issue is 12 years old at 43% vol. but independents offer a wide choice of 8- to 25-year-old and about a dozen vintages going back to 1948. It is the predominant malt at the heart of Chivas Regal and also graces a number of Seagram's other blends, including 100 Pipers

Aultmore Distillery

Location: **Keith, Banffshire**
Roads: **On A96 at turn-off to Buckie, B9016**
Visitors welcome by appointment
Tel: **01542-882762**

---

*T*his was one of the ventures of whisky entrepreneur Alexander Edward (see Benrinnes, Dallas Dhu, *et al*). The area around Aultmore has always been remote and sparsely populated, hence it was a thriving location of many smugglers' bothies. The numerous burns and the peat of the Foggie Moss were additional incentives to distil on the spot. Even today, Aultmore distillery is solitary in the landscape despite Keith's being only 2.5 miles distant. Not all smugglers were men and one of the better-known operators selling 'small-still' whisky to publicans in the surrounding towns was a woman called Jane Milne.

There is an old steam engine on display which supplied the distillery's power round the clock; to do so it was kept in continuous daily operation – except for repair and servicing periods – for the best part of 70 years. Whenever the engine was temporarily out of action the waterwheel, turned by lade-flow from a dam and which had previously supplied all power requirements, stood in.

The distillery was built in 1896 and did well immediately – so much so that extensions were built just two years later and production was doubled. Edward bought Oban distillery in the same year and made the two plants into a single limited company. The Pattison crash affected Edward both by Oban's having been a big supplier to them and also by the market's becoming flooded with Speyside malt whisky for the next few years. World War I, Prohibition in the US and the 1920s Depression finally brought about a sell-out to Dewar's of Perth, now a subsidiary of present owners, United Distillers. A second pair of stills was added to the original pair during the 1971 rebuilding work.

The Whisky

Aultmore is fresh and sweet with an edge of pleasantly astringent fruit and faint smoke. It is officially released at 12 years old and 43% vol., for the moment the only form in which it is available.

Auchroisk Distillery

Location: **Mulben, Banffshire**
Roads: **On A95 between Keith and Aberlour**
Tel: **01542-860333**

*T*he story goes that because someone stumbled across the well on the side of a steep ravine some time during the 1960s, the company decided to build the distillery. Perhaps that compresses events just a smidgen but good water is so important if you want to make good whisky, particularly if it flows at 2,000 gallons per hour. The company was Justerini & Brooks, owners of one of the world's top-selling blended Scotch brands, and they used water samples from the spring to run a test-distillation at their Glen Spey distillery at Rothes. Based on the results, J & B bought the well and the surrounding land, built a little stone hive with a lockable door over it and started planning.

Auchroisk (pronounced 'Ah-thrusk') was built to produce blending whisky for the J & B brand. The water was clear and soft, the malt lightly peated and the stills high in profile to produce the light, sweet estery spirit needed for the J & B house style. After eight years the first vintage was assessed and the company's best noses decided that Auchroisk was also an excellent single whisky – something that was a bonus and which, even if hoped for, could never have been planned. Thus the Singleton of Auchroisk came to be introduced (a single malt is an unblended malt whisky from a single distillery.)

Auchroisk was completed in 1975, a fresh and attractive complex of dark roofs

and white-harled walls with enough variation to its Lego-brick buildings to lighten
the visual impact of their overall bulk. In addition to its function as a distillery,
Auchroisk is an assembly point for all the other Highland distilleries' malts that are
used in J & B. They are vatted together according to the 'recipe' (secret, of course)
and tankered off to the group's blending centre near Glasgow where they meet up
with the Lowland, Islay, Campbeltown and grain whiskies of different ages that
comprise the final blend of over 40 whiskies. This returns to cask for a period of
marrying before going on to be bottled.

A steam engine, of the type formerly used in Highland distilleries to provide
power for the machinery, stands in the entrance hall. It used to be the main such
unit at Strathmill distillery. As already mentioned, the stills are high-necked to
produce a light, elegant spirit. The lyne-arms at the very top of the stills where the
vapours are funnelled over are horizontal, a detail that probably gives a final tweak to
the particularity of Auchroisk's whisky. There are four pairs of stills. The spring that
was found in such dramatic fashion and from which Auchroisk is made is called
Dorie's Well.

The Whisky

The Singleton of Auchroisk is medium in weight but offers an elegant range of fruit,
malt, smoke and herb flavours. It has a fine mellow texture and generous, smooth
length. The variegation of the whisky is definite but lightly drawn and to use too
much sherrywood would swamp this pleasant complexity. As a result it is largely ex-
Bourbon wood in which Auchroisk is matured, with a sherry finish grafted on by a
certain proportion of each batch spending the final one or two years in dry oloroso
sherry casks. The prevailing ages of each vintage since the first in 1986 has been 10
to 12 years and there is also an independent bottling of 12-year-old. Auchroisk is
used in the various J & B blends.

Above: The distillery has won architectural awards for its design, and trophies for its whisky.

Glentauchers Distillery

Location: **Mulben, Banffshire**
Roads: **On the A95 west of Keith**
No reception centre • Visitors welcome by appointment
Tel: **01543-860272**

*J*ames Buchanan, without any knowledge of the intricacies of distillation, set up his own company in 1884 to produce his own brand of whisky; his timing was spot-on because Scotch doubled in popularity over the following decade. He did not even have any capital, beginning with just credits from his subsequent partners in Glentauchers. He went on to spectacular success, was raised to the peerage and, even after giving away large amounts of his personal fortune, left £7 million pounds when he died at 85 years of age.

The distillery stands on a fringe of the Craigellachie Forest and was 'mothballed' in 1985. It has now been reopened under new owners, Allied Distillers, and started production again in 1989

James Buchanan & Co. Ltd., proprietors of the Black and White brand, were involved from the outset with Glentauchers. The distillery was completed in 1898 and in time a rail siding was completed. The water supply was copious so it was collected in a dam and then run through a turbine that powered everything. Substantial remodelling was carried out from 1923 to 1925, including a new spirit store designed by Charles Doig. The distillery was rebuilt in 1966 with extra stills.

The rebuilding in 1966 succeeded in creating a tidied-up exterior leaving some of the dark but shapely Victorian stone buildings. The floor maltings lost that function in 1969 and the space was given over to warehousing for casks. There are 3 wash and 3 spirit stills now in operation.

The Whisky

Glentauchers starts gently, develops some spicy, silky core and finishes quite strongly with smoky, mellow fruit and little medicinal flashes. There is no official bottling but 1979 vintage and 13-year-old were recently available from independents. The malt is used in Allied Distillers blends.

Above: Set in woodlands, the Mill of Towie has an upright, Victorian austerity.

Of interest around Keith

• An old stone **Packhorse Bridge** dating from 1609 was once the only means of crossing the River Isla to Fife Keith on the other bank. Witches used to be drowned in the Gaun Pot pool near the churchyard and Newmill just a mile to the north was the birthplace in 1794 of James Gordon Bennett, founder of the New York Herald newspaper.

• **Drummuir Castle** is a fine 19th-century mansion which incorporates a remarkable lantern tower. It also houses the **Clan Macduff Centre**.

• The **Mill of Towie** near Drummuir is a restored grain mill and produces oatmeal in the traditional manner. There is a mill-lade walk and the ponies are friendly.

• The **Grain Store**, also at Mill of Towie, has a working watermill.

• **Keith Whisky Barrel Cooperative** recycles the spent casks abandoned by the distilleries in the district. They are made into a wide range of products; even the sawdust gets used in local smokehouses for preparing smoked salmon.

Trail 4f • Around Tomintoul

Tomintoul, at 1160 feet (354m) above sea level the highest village in the Highlands, has a gridiron pattern and a central square as would be expected from a planned settlement. It is airy and pleasant, but in the years after the Duke of Gordon had established it the village was described as 'ugly-looking' and the inhabitants as 'outlandish ragamuffins'. It was built in 1754 after the Battle of Culloden when the Hanoverian military presence in the Highlands was still very strong, around an inn on the Lecht road, a military route that linked Fort George on the Moray coast with Edinburgh.

The first innkeeper was Janet Mackenzie, a colourful character who had travelled all over Europe and America as a cross between a military courtesan and an army wife. Tomintoul lay in the high country of the Glenlivet parish and illicit whisky was produced everywhere. Hence, Janet only agreed to take on the inn if the Duke of Gordon stopped 'the huts of Tomintoul from selling ale or whisky'. When the inn was well established Janet herself was probably one of the smugglers' best customers.

The Lecht road reaches over 2000 feet (610m) above sea level and has gradients of one in five (20%). It is the famous 'Cock Bridge to Tomintoul' route that, year in year out, is the first in the country to be blocked with snow as winter settles in. Janet Mackenzie brought up this fact when she was negotiating better leasing terms for her inn. She noted that the passing trade was not as much as she had expected and that 'the road is quite shut from the Month of January till the first of May yearly'.

Because of its remote location in the hills, the Tomintoul district's distillery projects were rare. Delnabo was one such, established in the late 1830s and bought in 1849 by George Smith of The Glenlivet fame. He dismantled Delnabo when he moved to his definitive distillery in 1858 and there was no other distillery around Tomintoul until the present one which was built in 1965.

Above: From the Lecht Road, the view is of open, uncompromising moorland.

4f

Tomintoul Distillery

Location: **Ballindalloch, Banffshire**
Roads: **On B9136, left-hand side, 6 miles north of Tomintoul**
Seasons: **Mid-Aug – early June except mid-Dec – mid-Jan**
Visitors are welcome by appointment only • Group bookings, max 10
No reception centre or shop • *Tel:* 01807-590274

*T*omintoul distillery was the venture of two Glasgow whisky broking firms, one of which owned the Real Mountain Dew whisky blend, which was well known a century ago. The distillery is modern, of course, and its design had enough merit to receive the approval of the Royal Fine Art Commission. It lies on a plateau 880 feet (268m) up in the hills below the village. During the winter the contractors always had two weeks' worth of building materials to hand so that work could continue if they were cut off from the outside world and purpose-built braziers enabled construction to go ahead even in 10 degrees of frost. Tomintoul was only the third new distillery to be built this century.

Production water is soft and is drawn from a spring. There are two pairs of stills, the second pair having been added in 1974. Stocks of whisky at the distillery now comprise 80,000 casks, going back to the first year of distillation in 1965.

The Whisky

Tomintoul is a medium-peated, light whisky with a pleasant bite and quite marked fragrance. It is fruity and spicy rather than malty and woody although these attributes do show through as background. The whisky was first released as a self whisky on the 10th anniversary of the distillery's opening. It is bottled by the proprietors at eight and 12 years and one of the independents recently came up with a 20-year-old. The Tomintoul make is used in all Whyte & Mackay blends.

The Glenlivet Distillery

Location: **Ballindalloch, Banffshire AB37 9DB**
Roads: **Off the B9008, 4 miles from Ballindalloch**
Seasons: **mid March – end October**
Hours: **10am – 4pm, Mon – Sat; 12.30 – 4.00 pm Sun;**
July – August open until 6.00pm daily
Explanation boards in French, German, Italian, Spanish and Japanese
Reception centre, shop, coffee shop • *Tel:* 01542-783220

Such was the reputation in the early 1800s of the illicit whisky produced in the Livet glen that it was sought by everyone in preference to any of the legally produced kind. There were over 200 unlicensed stills operating in Glenlivet at the time. What chance did the Excise have of convincing people of the immorality of smuggling if King George IV himself was continuously kept in good supply of illicitly produced Glenlivet whisky?

When the Excise Act was passed in 1823, a scramble of new distillery-building – 79 of them – got under way but George Smith's application for a licence was the first to be granted. It was a fact that came in useful nearly 60 years later when his company's product was challenged for the right to be regarded as *the* Glenlivet whisky. When the smugglers first 'went legal' there was unrest and some violence. Several distilleries were burned down and Smith himself reckoned that the pair of pistols that had been presented to him by the Laird of Aberlour saved his life on more than one occasion.

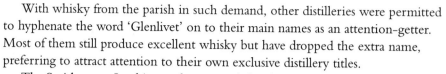

With whisky from the parish in such demand, other distilleries were permitted to hyphenate the word 'Glenlivet' on to their main names as an attention-getter. Most of them still produce excellent whisky but have dropped the extra name, preferring to attract attention to their own exclusive distillery titles.

The Smiths were Jacobites and supported the claims of Bonnie Prince Charlie to the British throne. Their real name was Gow but, in the bitter aftermath of the final Rebellion and Culloden, they adopted the less distinctive name of Smith for the sake of safety. They were farmers and illicit distillers – just like their neighbours around them – and when George Smith moved to Drumin farm in Glenlivet in 1817 he continued to distil without a licence.

His landlord, the Duke of Gordon, knew what was going on but he himself was about to play his part in revolutionising whisky production in Scotland. In 1820 he made a speech in Parliament which led directly to the Government's change in thinking that was reflected in the Excise Act of 1823. Once this was in place, he gave every assistance to Smith in the building of his legal distillery.

From 1849 Smith also operated a distillery called Delnabo, near Tomintoul (*qv*), which had been built in the 1830s. When his company moved to the present distillery site at Minmore in 1858, both Drumin and Delnabo were closed and dismantled.

The malt is centrally prepared but several kinds – some lightly peated, some more heavily peated – are used to give better dimension to aroma and texture. The old floor maltings are now just about all that is left of the original Minmore distillery; they were last used in 1966. The water is a mix of hard and soft. Since 1978 there have been four pairs of stills in operation.

The Whisky

The Glenlivet manages to show great finesse of aroma and weight yet delivers quite full, succulent, soft flavour. It is usually fruity, sherryish and sweet, gently smoky. The official releases are at 12, 18 (in the UK and USA) and 21 years old but, for such a widely popular and important malt, there is a vast choice of vintages going back to 1940 and pretty well every age, from 12 to 25 years old, from several independents.

Tamnavulin Distillery

Location: **Tomnavoulin, Ballindalloch, Banffshire • Roads: On the B9008
Reception centre open but distillery currently closed.**
Tel: **01807-590285**

*J*ust as there is a deep vocabulary in the Inuit language for snow in its many forms,
Scots Gaelic has many words for hill or mountain: meall, tom, beinn, creag, tor,
tulach, cnoc, stob, sgurr, sliabh and so on, to describe large, small, rounded, pointed
or other distinctive features. A 'tom' is a small, rounded hill and 'mhoulin' (compare
this with the French 'moulin') means a mill so this spot on a bank of the Livet is 'the
hill with the mill'. Mh is pronounced as 'v' in Gaelic hence the phonetic spelling
that also occurs in Islay's Lagavulin.

The mill at Tomnavoulin used to card the wool that the shepherds in the district
collected from the flocks scattered throughout the hills. It is now the distillery
reception centre and the waterwheel that powered the machinery has been restored.

The distillery dates from 1966 and there have been three pairs of stills in use
since the start. One fine aspect of modern distilleries is the efficiency they achieve.
In the stillhouse here the hot spirit running off the stills was used to preheat the
incoming batch of wash that is to be distilled. The water for whisky production
came from springs at Easterton but production has now temporarily ceased.

The Whisky

Tamnavulin matures rapidly and within a light, medium-weight structure, it shows
considerable mellowness and contented balance. Faint oakiness and fresh-fruit, malty
cleanness. The official bottlings are at 10 years and 40% or 43% vol. depending on
destination. The Stillman's Dram is the owners' special edition and is 25 years old, as
far back as it is possible to go with this youthful distillery.

Balmenach Distillery

Location: Cromdale, Morayshire • *Roads:* Off the A95 between Grantown and Bridge of Avon

*R*oad traffic, whether beast or man, has long passed to and fro through Cromdale, one of the crossing points of the Spey; on the hills above the village the Jacobites were defeated in a battle in 1690. Balmenach was one of the earliest of the new wave of distilleries sanctioned as a result of the new legislation in 1823. It is closely associated with Sir Robert Bruce-Lockhart whose book *Memoirs of a British Agent* had a big success on British television in telling the story of *Reilly Ace of Spies.*

Sir Robert wrote of spending the happiest days of his life as a boy in Cromdale and told the story of his farmer great-grandfather Macgregor who was visited by an Excise officer just after the Excise Act had been passed. As he was shown round the farm in a relaxed and friendly manner, the officer pointed to the outhouse where Macgregor produced his clandestine whisky and asked what it was for. 'That's just the peat-shed,' he replied. The officer said nothing and continued the tour. The two men drank some whisky, and then, as the officer rose to leave, he said quietly, 'If I were you, Mr. Macgregor, I'd take out a licence for yon peat-shed.'

Macgregor took the hint, which is why the licence to distil dates from 1824. Towards the end of the century when new-fangled electric light was starting to appear in the Highlands. Balmenach was distinctly old-fangled and water-powered. The whisky sold well and was exported to the colonies; in 1878 Queen Victoria enjoyed it during a stay at the Gairloch Hotel by Loch Maree.

The family survived the end-of-century whisky market collapse but production restrictions by the government during World War I to reserve cereals for foodstuffs finally led the Macgregors to sell on in the 1920s.

A Saladin Box malting system was installed in 1964 and used until the mid-1980s. There are three pairs of stills. The railway 'pug' engine that replaced the earlier locomotive worked at Balmenach for just over 30 years before the local railway line was axed by Dr Beeching in 1968. Unfortunately, with recessionary pressures once more touching the Scotch whisky industry, Balmenach was 'mothballed' in June, 1993.

The Whisky

A Speyside malt that combines elegance with full, round intensity of flavour. Dry, light malt and smoke, oaky musk. The official self whisky is 12 years old and 43% vol.

Left: A small locomotive shunted materials the mile to and from Cromdale station.

Of interest around Tomintoul

• **Tomintoul Museum** in the village square has a display on peat-working. There is also a reconstructed farmhouse kitchen with original domestic equipment.

• **Tomintoul Peat Moss** is worked two miles north of the village and a visitor trail allows access to see how the peat is extracted and the special equipment used.

• **Corgarff Castle** was built in the 1500s and figured prominently in both the 1715 and the 1745 Rebellions. It became a Hanoverian garrison in 1748 but latterly all there was for the redcoat soldiers to do was help chase whisky smugglers.

Left: With its star-shaped ramparts, Corgarff Castle stands guard over the great canyon of the Lecht Pass.

• The **Speyside Way** walking route has a spur that runs between Tomintoul and Ballindalloch, via The Glenlivet Distillery. Bus service allows access to intermediate points and ranger service on the Way provides information.

• **Lecht Iron Mine** in the hills was worked in the 1730s, the ore being taken over to Nethy Bridge where there was timber for smelting it. The old mine-house is still in place and there is an interpretative display and picnic area.

• An underground **Earth House**, associated with a Pictish construction, can be seen at Mains of Inverourie. It is a stone-lined granary and dates from about 1200 BC.

• **Tomintoul Highland Games** take place every year around mid July.

• The **Craggan Stones** in Strath Avon were used for clandestine open-air preaching when dissenters broke away from the Church of Scotland in 1843. The Free Church (the 'Wee Free') was formed as a result. The stones are at an alcove in the fence 300 metres south of Craggan Farm.

• **Scalan** was a secret seminary for Roman Catholic studies during the 18th century, a period when Catholicism was seen as tantamount to treason. The original house was burned down by Hanoverian troops and the present building dates from 1767.

• **Drumin Country Museum** displays household and farming equipment illustrating country life in north-east Scotland in the past.

Trail 5 / Central & Southern Highlands

From Glasgow or Edinburgh to Inverness

Introduction

This is a consistently rewarding whisky trail, not only because nearly all of the distilleries are visitable and in highly attractive settings, but also because the scenery through which you pass progresses from the lovely to the dramatic. It's well worth taking both the time and the trouble.

It is possible to embark upon this trail from either Glasgow or Edinburgh. Setting off in the west allows viewing Auchentoshan and Littlemill before moving on to Glengoyne; departure from the east, on the other hand, takes in Glenkinchie and its museum before heading for Glengoyne.

Above: The private collection of Sir William Burrell, a Glaswegian ship owner, was gifted to Glasgow and housed in a brand new building, designed by Barry Gasson and completed in 1983.

Auchentoshan Distillery

Location: **Dalmuir • *Roads:* On A82 by the Erskine Bridge over the River Clyde • Not open to visitors • *Tel:* 01389-878561**

Old Kilpatrick is where the Roman wall of Antoninus Pius, having crossed the narrowest part of Scotland, descended to the shore of the River Clyde at the north-western limit of the Roman Empire. It is a built-up area now so there is no trace above ground of the fort that stood here or the wall itself. Unlike Hadrian's stone wall to the south, the Antonine structure was made of turf and peat.

Auchentoshan is a Lowland malt but uses Highland water, as the source that is tapped for production is in the Kilpatrick Hills just to the north of the Highland Line. The malt is lightly peated and the spirit triple-distilled. Clydebank, the centre of the now-gone ship-building industry was heavily blitzed during the last war. The distillery dates from 1800 and has been in continual, rather than continuous, production ever since. A succession of operators ran it over the years. In the 1960s the Tennent brewery acquired it but the present owners are a smaller specialist independent company. The equipment is a mixture of ancient and modern with some of the wooden vats more than a century old. There is an old steam engine still in the distillery.

The Whisky

Auchentoshan is delicate and smooth with light, floral and fruity character. Slightly spicy and surprising fleshy. It is bottled as Select, 10 and 21 years old.

Of interest nearby

• **Ballantine's Whisky** Scottish base and grain whisky distilleries are located on the shore of the Firth of Clyde. Vast warehouses of maturing spirit are guarded by flocks of Chinese geese which are extremely noisy if anyone approaches their patch.

5

Littlemill Distillery

Location: Bowling, Dunbartonshire • Roads: Off the A814
Closed to visitors
Tel: 01389-874154

*I*f nearby Auchentoshan distillery lies beside the line of the old Roman wall, Littlemill is close by another long-distance engineering feat that crossed Scotland – the Forth and Clyde canal. The waterway was completed in 1790, just a dozen years after Littlemill itself is thought to have begun whisky production. The canal joins up with the Clyde at the village of Bowling where, in 1802, the world's first practical steamship, Symington's 'Charlotte Dundas', had its initial trials.

Littlemill, a Lowland malt, is a most interesting distillery in a pretty setting. With its probable foundation date of 1772, it is one of the three oldest distilleries in Scotland but it was also something of a test-bed for an American inventor who improved and rethought a number of aspects of malt whisky distillation.

Like its neighbour Auchentoshan, Lowland Littlemill uses water drawn from what is technically the Highlands to produce its whisky. The distillery shares a pipeline from the Auchentorlie Burn in the Kilpatrick Hills with British Rail and some small local shipyards. In fact, Littlemill's malt also comes from the other side of the Highland Line.

The first licensee after the facilitating 1823 Excise Act, Jane Macgregor, may well have been one of the earliest women distillers in Scotland. In 1875, just over 100 years after its inception, the distillery was rebuilt. In 1931, American Duncan

5

Left: After the distillation process, the spirit is drawn from the spirit vat into oak casks for maturation.

Thomas bought the distillery and began putting his ideas into practice - a process that was still going on 30 years later. He modified a Saladin Box system of malting and the double ventilation towers over a single drying kiln are a one-off in Scotland. The stills are copper but have outer skins of light aluminium as lagging and, most remarkably, they have rectifying columns instead of the swan-necks customary on pot-stills. In thus combining pot- and column-still elements, Thomas sought the capacity to 'tune in' at a lower or higher refining level and produce a hybrid spirit that would age faster. His technique has been embraced by Japanese distillers, who experiment with many different heads on identical pot-still bases to seek variations on given distilling themes.

The scale and pertness of the whitewashed distillery buildings are attractive, particularly in view of the nearness to the sprawl of Glasgow. Littlemill was triple-distilled until the 1930s, when it switched to the present double-distilled product. The distillery closed for some years during the 1980s before reopening under the ownership of Gibson International, the company having been formed by a management buy-out. The distillery ceased production in 1992 and Loch Lomond Distillers took over in 1994. The distillery remains closed, but supplies for bottling will be available for many years.

The Whisky

The variation in spirit types possible with Littlemill's single pair of stills meant that, for a while, the distillery produced three different malts. Dumbuck was a heavily peated whisky – most unusual for a Lowland distillery – and Dunglass had 'big' and full texture with a very light peat accompaniment. They were discontinued in the early 1970s. Today Littlemill is in the Lowland mould – delicate, gentle, sweet and malty.

Above: The village of Alloway (left) was the birthplace of Robert Burns (this portrait is by Alexander Nasmyth, and can be seen in the National Portrait Gallery of Scotland).

Of interest nearby

• **Hill House** in Helensburgh was a 'total design' commission for his home given to Charles Rennie Mackintosh by the Glasgow publisher Blackie. Everything is integrated and complementary, including the furniture. The windows are ingenious; they swivel as well as moving up and down. It all looks so *avant garde*, yet it dates from 1902. Visitors welcome. (Upper Colquhoun Street.) Helensburgh was also the birthplace of John Logie Baird, the inventor of television.

• **Loch Lomond Distillery** is sited less attractively than its name suggests, but it produces a fine light Highland malt called Inchmurrin, named after the largest island in the Loch.

• **The Burrell Collection** in parkland at Pollok, near Glasgow, is one of the world's greatest private collections of art objects, and was bequeathed to the citizens of Glasgow.

• **Charles Rennie Mackintosh:** Worth visiting in Glasgow are the School of Art designed inside and out by Mackintosh; the 'Art-Lover's House' in Bellahouston Park (designed by Mackintosh in 1901 and built in 1989); and the Willow Tearoom, preserved within a Glasgow store.

• The **Johnnie Walker Bottling Plant** at Kilmarnock welcomes visitors and there are daily tours of the bottling lines.

• **Croy 'Electric' Brae** at Dunure embodies an optical quirk of the lie of the roadway, which gives the illusion of cars moving without power. A car put into neutral at a given spot will apparently move uphill under its own power although the slope is, in fact, downhill.

• **Robert Burns** is associated with many sites in Ayrshire; start with his birthplace at Alloway, just south of Ayr.

• **Culzean Castle**, designed by Robert Adam, sits on a precipice on the coast 12 miles south of Ayr. Its grounds are now a country park.

Glenkinchie Distillery

Location: **Pencaitland, East Lothian EH34 5ET**
Roads: **Off the A6903, off the A68 Edinburgh to Jedburgh**
Seasons: **All year, 9.00 - 4.00pm, Mon - Fri and**
Sat/Sun April - October
Group bookings by appointment
Reception centre, shop and exibition • *Tel:* 01875-340451

*E*ast Lothian has been something of a punchbag over the centuries; it lies on the route that invading English armies tended to favour and the open rolling countryside made it useful for battle when the Scottish forces rallied in defence. Places like Haddington have been burned many times by visiting generals and Berwick changed hands between the two countries so often that today the town is in England while the county is in Scotland.

There is just a frisson of an impression that you have gone back a little in time when you drop into the green dell that contains Glenkinchie. The baize-smooth bowling green and inviting little pavilion are just as they would have been years ago when they formed the social centre for the families of the distilling community hidden in the gentle hills behind Edinburgh. The 'kinchie' element of the name derives from the de Quincey family, who owned the land hereabouts in the 14th century and the Kinchie Burn still flows through the distillery.

The top-grade barley grown in the Lothians is the direct legacy of the Society of Improvers of Knowledge of Agriculture, a revolutionary 18th-century body that put

5

Above: All the equipment used in the distillery has to be kept clean to ensure that no extraneous flavours taint the spirit.

Scotland in the forefront of the European farming scene at the time. The society was founded by John Cockburn of the village of Ormiston just across the fields from Glenkinchie, whose whisky production began as a part-time operation on the Rate brothers' farm near Pencaitland. From 1825 the distillery was called Milton and in 1837 the name was changed to Glenkinchie. The next owner of the farm did not distil and the buildings became a sawmill, but whisky production began again in 1881. In the 1890s the distillery was rebuilt and became a founder company of the DCL, forerunners of today's owners, United Distillers.

The old maltings is now the Museum of Malt Whisky Production, with an excellent collection of old and traditional implements and tools that were used in Scottish distilleries. There are barley-scoops on wheels that look like dolls' prams; espadrille-like canvas boots that maltmen wore to walk about without damaging the malt on the floor; and many other fascinating artefacts. Many were ingeniously thought out, like the copper 'dogs' – containers that were used to smuggle stolen spirit out of the distillery. Some were simple tubes slim enough to be dipped and filled through the bung-hole of a cask and then hung by a piece of string inside a

Above: The low, open-plan building that used to be the floor maltings at Glenkinchie now houses the Museum of Malt Whisky Production.

trouser-leg on the way out from work; others were more elaborate, such as the breastplate shaped to the curve of a torso and double-skinned like a hot-water bottle, which could be hung under a shirt with string tied around the carrier's neck.

There is a single pair of large stills, each with sighting windows to double-check, if need be, what stage the boiling has reached. In the past, a wooden ball used to hand on the still from a piece of string; when swung against the side of the vessel, the note indicated to an experienced ear how full or empty it was. The stills have unusually angled lyne-arms at the top of thickish necks. A rather unusual worm-tub is still used to condense the spirit: it is two storeys high, the tub is cast-iron and the worm itself is a rectangular spiral instead of the customary circular shape.

In horse-and-cart days, majestic large-hoofed Clydesdales pulled the dray-carts at DCL distilleries all around the country. Those that worked in Glasgow used to be sent to Glenkinchie for their 'summer holidays', where they could canter and amble without the restriction of the carts. In the 1950s, the manager also ran the Glenkinchie beef herd which won the fatstock Supreme Championship at Smithfield, Birmingham and Edinburgh in three successive years, plus many other individual show championships. What an advertisement for the quality of the cattle feeds made from the malting and mashing processes!

The Whisky

Glenkinchie is light, soft, round and sweetish, although it is drier than most other Lowland malts. Some smoke, nutmeg and bite. It is issued at 10 years and 43% vol., but there are some vintages from the 1970s available from independents.

5

Left: The façade of the Scotch Whisky Heritage Centre in Edinburgh gives little hint of the exciting displays depicting the history and production of the spirit.

Of interest nearby

• The Scotch Whisky Heritage Centre in Edinburgh's Royal Mile below the Castle has the sights, sounds and smells of the history of whisky production. You move in a whisky-barrel car through tableaux from history, with commentary available in seven different languages.

• **Drambuie Liqueur** is produced and bottled at Kirkliston. The story of its origins is a romantic one, involving Bonnie Prince Charlie and a Skyeman, John Mackinnon, descendants of whom still run the company. Visit the plant to hear more and watch how the liqueur is made. Tel: 0131-333 3531 for details.

• Visit the plant that produces **Glayva Liqueur** – Edinburgh's other international whisky liqueur. Tel: 0131-554 4404.

• **Winton House** near Haddington is a masterpiece of Scottish Renaissance architecture. Fine furniture, ornate ceilings and intricate stone carvings.

• **The Heritage of Golf Museum** at Gullane has a good collection of golfing memorabilia. Ask them if golf really did originate in Scotland and not in Holland, as some evidence now seems to show.

• **The Museum of Flight** at East Airfield has an extensive aircraft collection and displays of the history of flight. New Zealanders still think their own man, Richard Pearse, beat the Wright brothers to it; he just didn't bother to write down the date of his flight at the time!

• The **Scottish Mining Museum** at the former Lady Victoria colliery has ex-miners as guides. They tell the story of a site that has been mined for 800 years.

Glengoyne Distillery

Location: **Dumgoyne, nr. Killearn, Stirlingshire G63 9LB**
Roads: **On A81, 500 metres south of junction with A875**
Seasons: **Easter – November, tours on the hour 10am – 4pm,**
Mon – Sun and Tues / Thurs evenings;
December – March, Mon–Fri 10am–4pm.
Telephone for information about evening tutored tasting –
Group bookings, max 50; larger parties by appointment
Video and booklets in French, German, Italian, Spanish and Japanese
Reception centre, heritage room and shop
Tel: **01360-550254** *Fax:* **01364-550094**

Snug at the bottom of a mare's-tail burn that falls down the side of Dumgoyne Hill, Glengoyne is a pretty, endearing distillery that just begs to be visited. Behind the main buildings is a secret little glen where the final 60-foot (18m) of the burn splashes into a pool. Visitors sip their dram overlooking it all after their tour round the distillery. Loch Lomond lies to the north-west and 15th-century Duntreath Castle with its mediaeval stocks and dungeons is just down the road.

Every distillery had its live-in Excise Officer until very recently. The Officer at Glengoyne at the tail-end of last century was Arthur Tedder who later gave important evidence at the 1908 Royal Commission which decided whether grain spirit qualified as whisky. He became the Chief Inspector of Excise and was later knighted; his son, who had grown up at Glengoyne, was made Air Chief Marshal of the Royal Air Force after a brilliant war record as deputy supreme commander under Eisenhower. When made a baron he chose the title of Baron Tedder of

Glenguin, the old spelling of Glengoyne.

The distillery emerged directly from the illicit distilling activity that covered the floor of Strathblane and the Small Stills permitted by law and mostly held by the landowners in the district. The first Glengoyne distillery in 1833 belonged to the Edmonstones of Duntreath Castle and probably displaced a Small Still on the same site. The distillery came into the hands of Lang Brothers, the present owners, in 1872. Glengoyne is a Highland malt.

There are three stills, one of which is getting on for 30 years old (on average stills last about 20 years). The other two are six years old. This does not mean triple-distillation, although it used to be carried out at Glengoyne. Now the two spirit stills have been made of a size that enables them together to take a single batch of distillate from the wash still. The rapidity or otherwise of distillation is an important factor in the quality of spirit – the slower the better; Glengoyne's distillation rate is said to be very slow.

The lack of space at Glengoyne meant its going over to buying in malt as early as 1910; it also meant that the filling store had to be across the road from the distillery. Rather than have the men dodging traffic as they trundled casks across the busy road, a copper pipe was installed under the roadway and the whisky is pumped direct from the distillery to the filling store.

Before a rebuilding programme in 1966, Glengoyne was one of the smallest distilleries in Scotland. Today it is still small and attracts a lot of visitors. The distillery has its own helipad and as many as six helicopters a day land unloading customers, agents and even tourists on tight schedules.

Opposite: Visitors to Glengoyne may have the chance to taste the spirit overlooking the waterfall that brings the burn down from the secret glen. Right: A cooper at work, sealing the gap between the cask head and the staves. Below: Fire is used to toast the casks before the new spirit is added.

The Whisky

Glengoyne is light, soft and approachable in style. It has a fine, forward maltiness with fruit-and-nut finish. The attractive medium-depth complexity of Glengoyne comes through at least partly because there is no peat-reek whatsoever in the whisky. The malt is dried without peat smoke, leaving the herby, botanical notes unmasked. The plain-oak maturation also helps this, although a proportion of the whisky does come from sherrywood. There are 10, 12 and 17-year-old editions and the occasional 'one-off' like the recent Christmas Day, 1967 issue which was distilled on Christmas morning of that year. Independent bottlings are rare.

5

*Above: As the
mountains close in
around the top of Loch
Lomond, the pier at
Inversnaid provides a
delightful viewpoint.
Left: Luss is a scenic
village, with its own
pier where you can take
a steamer up the Loch.*

Above: With a wintery mist and the sun set low in the sky it is easy to see how mysterious legends grew up.

Of interest nearby

• **Luss**, on the west bank of Loch Lomond, is very beautiful. Wednesday to Friday you might catch them filming the *Take the High Road* TV serial, but the walking and sailing are excellent too. One of the delightful islands in the loch hosts a naturist club and pleasure boats passing the spot are said to list to one side as passengers crowd the landward rail for a glimpse of movement onshore.

• **Inversnaid** is the old steamer terminal on the east bank of Loch Lomond where it begins to narrow. The road stops there so it is tranquil and relaxing.

Deanston Distillery

Location: **Doune, Perthshire**
Roads: **On south bank of River Teith two miles from Doune**
Closed to visitors • *Tel:* 01786-841422

Doune is an interesting little place. It is famous in today's antiques world for its 17th-century pistols, a local industry that specifically served cattle-drovers since the town was a thriving cattle market at the time. Doune Castle is a well-preserved example of the need in 14th-century Scotland to combine military and domestic elements in the same buildings. The comedy movie *Monty Python and the Holy Grail* was shot here. As was *The Bruce*, in 1996.

Whisky, too, has an interesting historical connection at Doune. The distillery building was designed by Richard Arkwright, the inventor of the spinning frame that caused riots and redundancy among Lancashire cotton-workers in the 1760s.

The Arkwright cotton mill that Highland Deanston distillery occupies was built in 1785 but much of the structural work was added later in 1836. This includes the extraordinary vaulted weaving shed which is now a maturation warehouse. The conversion to distillation was carried out in 1966 and included taking out four internal floors to accommodate the stills and other machinery. The distillery was silent from 1982 but changed hands and is now back in production again through an independent firm, Burn Stewart. They have already won export achievement and company-turnaround awards so the future looks bright. An interesting aspect is the use of water-powered turbines as the energy source, something that was a familiar sight to those working Scotland's distilleries a century ago.

There are two pairs of stills which have quite narrow necks with ball-shaped bulges and slightly upward sloping Lyne arms to give lighter spirit through reflux. The enclosed, riverside warehouses, including one that lies beneath a garden, give excellent conditions of constant humidity and temperature for ageing malt whisky.

The Whisky

Deanston is elegant, sweet and smooth. The main flavours are herby maltiness and pert fruit with a fringe of faint smoke from the lightly peated malt. Lissom, easy, pleasing finish. A new Deanston will soon be launched as a 5-year old old. There are 12, 17 and 25-year-old editions from the proprietors although, since the company only recently came into being, these distillations were made by the previous owners. It remains to be seen if the style of the self whisky evolves differently in the years to come. There is also some 14-year-old Deanston available from private bottlers.

Of interest nearby

• The **Tailor's Bridge** over the Teith dates from 1535 and commemorates a rich man's vindictiveness to the ferryman who worked the crossing-point. A traveller, who was tailor to King James IV, wanted to underpay the ferryman who, predictably, refused to transport him. To gain revenge, the tailor paid for the bridge to be built so that he would be forced out of business.

• **Blair Drummond Safari Park** has a good drive-through live-animal habitat; check that you have some spare windscreen wipers in the boot before you go!
• **Doune Motor Museum** is part of the Doune Castle complex.

Left: The elephants seem surprisingly at home in the grounds of Blair Drummond Safari Park.

5

Tullibardine Distillery

Location: **Blackford, Perthshire**
Roads: **Off the A9 near Auchterarder**
Closed. No visitors

*A*uchterarder was torched in the wake of the Battle of Sheriffmuir which ended the 1715 Jacobite Rebellion; the Highlanders' swords had to be hidden in the roof thatch for another 30 years before the next real opportunity would present itself. The town was also the scene in 1843 of the split within the established Scottish Protestant Church which led to the formation of the Free Church of Scotland, known familiarly as the Wee Free.

There was a Tullibardine distillery in the Blackford area in the late-1790s but it did not last long. Its successor took a long time to appear, and then it was in the shell of an old brewery that goes as far back as the year 1488 when it produced a special ale for the coronation of King James IV at Scone.

The brewery was redesigned in 1949 by William Delme-Evans, architect of Jura and Glenallachie distilleries. He was the partner of a retired Excise officer in setting up the venture but it proved too much of a financial drain and in 1953 it was sold on. Eventually it came into the present owners' hands and in 1974 the distillery was rebuilt. There are two pairs of stills, while water for both whisky making and cooling comes from the Danny Burn.

5

The Whisky

Tullibardine, a Highland malt, shows great delicacy in its presentation of a fruity, spicy taste with a herby edge. There is malt, too, and bite in the background. Medium weight. The regular bottling is 10 years old and 40/43% vol. but the proprietors also do an older edition, the Stillman's Dram, at 25 years. One of the independents recently offered 27-year-old.

Left: Castle Campbell, 'The Castle of Gloom' has a well-preserved 15th-century tower, surrounded by later buildings. Above: Within relatively easy reach of both Glasgow and Edinburgh, Gleneagles Hotel and golf course are renowned internationally.

Of interest nearby

• **Gleneagles** – the magnificent hotel and the classic golf courses - lies just to the east.

• **Castle Campbell** has an imposing location on a spur of rock overlooking the Dollar glen and all the way to the flatlands of the Forth. It was built in the 15th century by the first Earl of Argyll and burned by Cromwell. It is a good example of a late mediaeval fortified house.

• **Muthill Church** is a ruin but its graveyard has headstones carved with various old symbols of local trades.

5

Glenturret Distillery

Location: **Glenturret, Crieff, Perthshire PH7 4HA**
Roads: **Off the A85 near Crieff**
Seasons: **Jan & Feb, 11.30am – 4.00pm Mon – Fri last tour 2.30pm;
Mar – Dec, 9.30am – 6.00pm Mon – Sat. Last tour 4.30pm. Sun from
12 noon • Groups over 40 by appointment
Reception centre, exhibition, shop and restaurants**
Tel: **01764-656565**

Crieff was the great mediaeval cattle tryst of Scotland with herds converging from 25 different locations in all directions – from the Highlands, Lowlands and Borders – to be bought and sold. It was later a Victorian spa town and in the 18th century illicit distilling was carried out almost with impunity in the hills all around. Glenturret Distillery is the oldest distillery in Scotland; it dates from 1775 and illicit stills on the site go back as far as 1717.

The first named distiller at Glenturret (then named Hosh) was recorded in 1818 and there was already another distillery nearby which, in 1826, adopted the Glenturret name. It eventually faded from the scene and in 1875 the Hosh distillery became definitively Glenturret.

Distilling was stopped in 1921 and the distillery used only for warehousing whisky until 1927. In 1929 the distillery was dismantled and turned over to farm storage. In 1957, James Fairlie began a three-year drive to revive Glenturret as a

Above right: The Visitors' Centre at Glenturret, complete with pristine barrels, is one of the top attractions in the area.

distillery and today it is again one of the Highlands' established malt whiskies.

The distillery buildings form a line along the base of a little wooded ravine and the scale of operation is very small. Total production staff is six – a mashman and stillmen. Tasks that are done automatically in larger distilleries are still done by hand here – rather laboriously but deliberately so – in order to recreate the kind of routines that were worked a century ago. There is an old Porteous grinding mill for making the grist and a single pair of stills.

The Whisky

One of the interesting aspects of Glenturret is that there are so many variations on the theme that it is difficult to think of any one's being the 'standard' issue. The 12-year-old at 40% vol. shows full aroma, round succulent roasted-nuts flavour and a big, velvety, oaky finish. Ages go from 12- to 25-years old; vintages go back to the 1960s; there is a 5,000-day bottling; cask-strength bottlings; ex-Bourbon and sherry bottlings. There are also independent bottlings.

Of interest nearby

• Astronaut Alan Bean carried a strip of Bean tartan with him when he landed on the moon. He presented it to the 13th-century **Church of St. Bean** at Fowlis Wester, which now displays the strip of cloth.
• **Old Stocks** which were used for public admonition until 1816 can be seen outside the town hall in Crieff High Street.
• The old **Mercat Cross** in Crieff turned out to be much older than most people realised. Long after it had been installed in the market square it was realised that it was a 10th-century Celtic cross stone slab with carved runic knots.

Aberfeldy Distillery

Location: **Aberfeldy, Perthshire PH15 2EB**
Roads: **On A827 by Aberfeldy**
Open all year: **Easter – October, 9.30am – 4.30pm Mon – Fri;**
November – March, by appointment
Group bookings by appointment
Reception centre, shop and exhibition • *Tel:* 01887-820330

*A*berfeldy is an attractive, typically Highland town with an elegant road bridge built by General Wade; this one is special, however, having been designed by William Adam. The town was visited by Robert Burns (who then wrote his song *The Birks o' Aberfeldy*). The distillery lies in a beautiful setting on the bank of the River Tay with woodland close by which has a population of rare red squirrels.

The distillery belonged to Dewar's the Perth blending firm and their bottled whisky was already doing well enough by the 1880s for a London office to be opened. In 1892, regarding the world as his oyster, Tommy Dewar set off on a two-year world tour to promote his whisky. He came back with 32 new agents in 26 different countries. He used to get his share of requests for money, and on the occasions that they were made face to face with him, he would hand over a card which read, 'I have given up lending money for some time, but I don't mind having a drink. Make it a Dewar's.' He was later the third person in the UK to own a car (after Thomas Lipton, the tea and groceries magnate, and the Prince of Wales). Both of the Dewar brothers became Lords, Forteviot and Dewar being the names they chose.

The project by John Dewar's of Perth to build Aberfeldy got under way in 1896 but it was in the difficult year of 1898 that production actually began. An earlier Aberfeldy distillery had been set up but it only lasted a couple of decades and Pitilie, founded in 1825, was also short-lived. The Dewar operation was on the same burn, the Pitilie, as well as on the Aberfeldy/Perth railway line, a factor that was important in making the distillery viable. Dewar's acquired six other malt whisky distilleries between 1919 and 1923, all of which they took with them when they became partners of DCL in 1925, and, in the 1980s, joined United Distillers

The still house and tun-room were rebuilt in 1973 using the original stonework. The old kiln with its pagoda roof is still in position but it now contains a production unit for pot ale syrup, a high-protein cattle feed made from the lees of the first distillation. Medium-peated malt is used from the company maltings. There are two pairs of stills.

The Whisky

Aberfeldy, a Highland malt, fills out from a lightly peaty aroma to a big, fairly concentrated smoky, tangy-fruit flavour. Some attractive wood and flowery sweetness. It is officially available at 15 years old and 43% vol. with some vintages going back to the 1970s from the independents.

Of interest nearby

• **Castle Menzies** at Weem is an excellent example of the unique architectural style that developed in the Scottish fortified house. It has a museum.
• **Aberfeldy Water Mill** is a fetching water mill of 1825 vintage now restored to

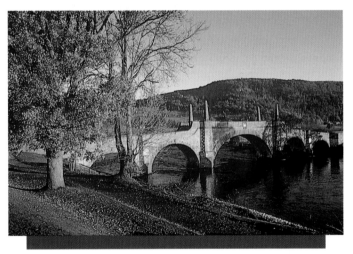

Left: The bridge over the Tay at Aberfeldy shows the elegant, classic design of William Adam.

full working status. There is a little museum and theatre where the story is told of traditional meal-milling and its effect on the community.
• **Dunkeld** means 'Fort of the Celts' and it goes back to 729 AD when it was a place of safety for fugitive monks. The roofless cathedral spanned 500 years of construction. The National Trust's Little Houses are an intriguing group of town cottages restored to 18th-century authenticity.

Edradour Distillery

Location: **Pitlochry, Perthshire PH16 5JP**
Roads: **On A924 2 miles from Pitlochry** • *Seasons:* **March – October**
*Hours:***9.30am – 5pm, Mon – Sat; Sun.12.00 – 5.00pm**
Nov – Feb, shop only • **Group bookings by appointment, max 50**
Reception centre and shop *Tel:* **01796-472095** *Fax:* **01796 472002**

This is the smallest distillery in Scotland. The setting is absolutely idyllic and its appearance makes it almost good enough to eat. With its brightly painted miniature vats, its picket fences and the pert burn tumbling down the middle of the grounds it is like something from the film *Brigadoon*. In fact Edradour was the main location setting in a television drama called *King's Royal*, which told the story of a Scottish distilling family.

But it is a working distillery and the production staff was increased by 50 per cent not so long ago – there are now three of them. It is the last example of the Perthshire farm-distilleries and the old-fashioned equipment has been retained as much as possible. The Morton refrigerator used for cooling the wort (*see glossary*) is the last in the industry. The scale of operation is such that Edradour may be genuinely regarded as a hand-crafted malt whisky.

This is distilling in miniature. Edradour's stills are the smallest legally permissable; any smaller, the Excise's thinking goes, and they become easily concealable in bushes, hayricks or peat-sheds. It takes those three members of staff a year to produce what a standard Speyside distillery can distil in a week. A week's work at Edradour yields about 12 casks of spirit at 70% vol.

The distillery first appears in records in 1837 but the owners believe it dates from 1825. There are indications of a mill nearby that goes back even earlier, probably a *bona fide* operation that also covertly catered for the local 'black pots' as the small,

Left: The picturesque mash-tuns from Scotland's smallest distillery.

unlicensed stills were called. The distillery was named Glenforres for a while. The water runs over granite through peat and the barley is locally produced.

Production methods are practically unchanged since 1825. There is one pair of stills – there certainly would not be room for any more. The spirit condenses in worm-tubs cooled by the distillery burn. When Excisemen found illicit stills in the past, the first piece of equipment they destroyed was the worm because the hollow, spiral shape was so difficult to make and replace.

During Prohibition in the US, the owner of the distillery, William Whiteley, supplied whisky to the smugglers running alcohol into the cities. Whiteley had specially toughened square bottles designed for the rough treatment consignments usually received, torpedoes carrying 40-gallon loads of Scotch were fired on to Long Island beaches at night from ex-Navy torpedo boats and cases of his House of Lords brand were taken into New York under tons of smelly rubbish in barges. Home deliveries were even made, usually by limousine or hearse. Neighbours must have witnessed many a puzzlingly joyful bereavement in those days.

The Whisky

Edradour is a sherry-style Highland malt and is aged exclusively in ex-oloroso sherry casks from Jerez in Spain. The aroma is rich in smoke and fruit with a spicy-sweet, almond/walnut flavour. The sherry tones are quiet but the texture is quite big and weighty. The official issue is 10 years old with variable strength. Sparing, almost nominal, amounts of Edradour go into House of Lords and Clan Campbell blends.

Of interest nearby

• **Blair Castle** is up the road near the feudal village of Blair Atholl and is the seat of the Dukes of Atholl. Parts of the castle date from the 1200s, Cromwell blew it up in the 1600s and it was the last castle on British soil to be besieged. The Duke is the only person in the UK permitted to have a private army, the Atholl Highlanders. Blair Castle is the gathering place for members of the Keepers of the Quaich, the worldwide society of personalities, businessmen and writers who honour the heritage of Scotch whisky.

5

Blair Athol Distillery

Location: **Pitlochry, Perthshire PH16 5LY**
Easter-end Sept. Mon - Sat. 9.00 am - 5.00 pm Sunday 12 -5.00pm
October - Easter Mon - Fri 9.00 am - 5.00 pm
Groups welcome, booking essential
Reception centre, shop, exhibition and coffee shop
Tel: **01796-472234** *Fax:* **01796-473292**

*B*lair Atholl, the village, is not where you find Blair Athol, the distillery (note the spellings), which in fact is on the main road that runs through the town of Pitlochry about seven miles or so to the south. Pitlochry is a comfortable little resort, always busy and popular both for overnight stops and longer stays. Birnam Wood, with King Duncan's castle and other Macbeth associations, is just to the north. During a stay at Kinnaird Cottage near Moulin, Robert Louis Stevenson wrote some of his short stories, including *The Merry Men* and *Thrawn Janet.*

Blair Athol is another of the handful of distilleries that were founded in the 18th century, albeit in the final few years. The works set up in 1798 either did not last very long or it was an illicit operation left undocumented. Thus it was either revived or first licensed in 1825, when the new licensing laws had been passed. Blair Athol was bought, along with Dufftown distillery (*qv*), by blenders Arthur Bell in 1933 but stayed out of production until 1949, when it was rebuilt.

Blair Athol has its own burn, the Allt na Dour, which runs through the distillery. Peat used to be brought from as far afield as Orkney but the malted barley is now lightly peat-smoked to Blair Athol's specification by the group's own central malting operations. Storage space is limited at the distillery and malt is usually delivered twice daily.

The original pair of stills was supplemented by a second pair in 1973. The standard milling machine used in distilleries is a Porteous – look out for its rich Burgundy-coloured paint as you see round – and the belt-driven model at Blair Athol was used from 1934 until recently. The distillery is highly energy-efficient, carrying out production at only 60 per cent of the power-consumption levels typical in the industry.

Spirit intended for sale as a single malt is matured in Blair Athol's old traditional-style warehouses; spirit for blending in Bell's blends is also matured in the other distillery warehouses; and the spirit that is sold into the open whisky market (about half) is filled into wood and tankered off to destination when required.

The Whisky

Blair Athol is fresh and gently peaty with aroma and flavour which become quite resonant and lengthy at the finish. There is a tangy, spicy-fruit quality to the core flavour. The self whisky is 12 years old and 43% vol. from Bell's but independents offer older editions up to 25 years old. The distillery and the whisky are closely identified with Bell's blends and the make figures prominently in them.

Of interest nearby

• The **Fish Ladder** is an artificial waterfall with glass-fronted viewing chambers, which give visitors underwater views of salmon and other fish making their way up

and down the river that runs through the town.
• **Loch Faskally** is a 'new' loch formed by the hydro-electric system's dam at which there is a visitor centre.
• The **Festival Theatre** began in 1951 in a tent and is now a permanent theatre running repertory programmes throughout the year.

Above: Well kept gates control the flow of water over a weir in the distillery grounds.

5

Dalwhinnie Distillery

Location: **Dalwhinnie, Inverness-shire PH19 1AB**
Roads: **Off main A9 road north**
Seasons: **All year, 9.30am – 5pm, Mon – Fri**
Group bookings by appointment
Reception centre, shop and exhibition • *Tel:* 01528 522 208

*I*n many ways Dalwhinnie is more like a fort guarding the Khyber Pass than a distillery on one of the country's main roads. It is the highest distillery in Scotland, sitting at over a 1000 feet (350m) above sea level yet at the very bottom of an enormous exposed bowl of encircling mountains. In winter the wind scours the slopes unchecked and snow drifts so deeply that distillery workers have on occasion had to go to work leaving from the first-floor windows of their cottages.

The distillery is also an official meteorological station and the manager must take daily data from the Stevenson screen in the grounds no matter the weather. Sometimes it can be quite a fight. 'Dalwhinnie' means 'meeting place' and it was the junction of the main cattle droving routes from the north and west of the Highlands. Herds and herdsmen would rest here before tackling the final surge to the great cattle trysts in the Lowlands. Here too General Wade's military road divided to follow similar directions and the line of the road actually runs through the grounds of the distillery. Many battles were fought in this very amphitheatre, the advantage of the home-fixture very much with the clansmen. Cromwell's Ironsides were sent packing from here and Bonnie Prince Charlie and his men camped on the moors behind the distillery on the way south after his Standard was raised at Glenfinnan.

The distillery buildings are a visual pun, their black roofs and white walls referring to the Black & White blended whisky brand for which licensees, Buchanan's, are well known. The original name was the Strathspey distillery, built this high at 1073 feet (327m) in 1898 to have the closest access to the uncontaminated, cold water of Lochan an Doire-uaine. Of course this was the worst possible time to be building a distillery and the company went into liquidation almost immediately. The name was changed to Dalwhinnie by the following owners and specialist distillery architect, Charles Doig of Elgin, was brought in to upgrade the buildings and layout. Dalwhinnie closed for several years after a serious fire in 1934, a time when there was still no electricity in the distillery or the village and paraffin lamps were still in use. Nor was there a telephone.

The distillery is surrounded by vast peat deposits, an important amenity in the early days, but its malt comes pre-peated from central maltsters now and has light-to-medium reek. Most of the storage capacities for raw materials are large making it possible for the distillery to produce for over a month if need be when it is snowed in. There is a single pair of stills and the original worm-tubs were from an old distillery at Kingussie.

The Whisky

Dalwhinnie, in contrast to the wild and punishing country that yields it, is a soft and amenable malt. It is aromatic, shows delicately smoky peat and closes smoothly with some rich complexity. Dalwhinnie is officially 15 years old and 43% vol. but independents occasionally have vintages going back to 1970. The make goes into the Buchanan range of blends.

Above: Whatever the weather, it is the duty of the manager to take daily readings of pressure, temperature and rainfall for the Meteorological Office.

Of interest nearby

• **Dalwhinnie Hotel** dates from 1729 and was a pretty basic inn when Queen Victoria visited in 1861 after a 13-hour journey. She took a dim view of the 'two miserable, starved, Highland chickens' that were served as her main course. Things have had plenty of time to improve by now. She had come close to buying an estate near here before finally deciding that Balmoral was the one she liked. If you stay overnight there may well be red deer in the garden when you look out of the window in the morning.

• **Ruthven Barracks**, windowless and gaunt on their natural platform in open country near Kingussie, were built by the government after the 1715 Rebellion and destroyed by the Highlanders after the failure of the 1745.

• The **Highland Folk Museum** at Kingussie is stuffed with data and artefacts about Highland life and history. It lays on exhibitions, both indoors and outdoors, and runs a programme of live demonstrations of country skills.

• **Stag's Breath** whisky liqueur is produced at Newtonmore on the main road north towards Inverness. Tel: 01540-673733 for information about visits.

Above: Dalwhinnie is close by Loch Ericht, to the west of the Grampian Mountains.

5

Tomatin Distillery

Location: **Tomatin, Inverness-shire IV13 7YT**
Roads: **On the A9, 16 miles south of Inverness**
Seasons: **Open all year. Mon – Fri 9.00am – 5.00pm (last tour 3.30pm)**
Sat: May – Oct 9.00am – 1.00 pm (last tour 12.00)
Groups must book in advance • No admission charge
Distillery tour, displays, tastings • *Tel:* 01808-511444

This is Scotland's largest Malt whisky distillery producing 12 million litres a year and, at 1028 ft (313m), the third-highest. It is a rather exposed, treeless stretch of country yet in prehistoric times it was thick with pine forest. During the excavation of the 30-foot-deep (9m) cutting for the railway here, successive levels of the remains of pine trees were discovered; the line rises to the summit pass of the Slochd not much farther to the south.

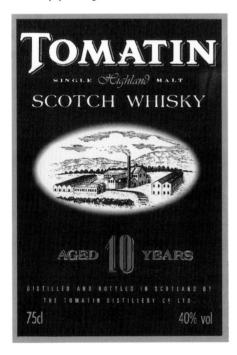

As a distilling site, illicit or otherwise, Tomatin goes back to the 15th century but the present operation dates from 1897 when the distillery-building bubble was just about to burst. As late as 1956 it had just two stills but in a major expansion programme in 1973, the capacity was boosted from 12 stills to a mighty total of 23. Tomatin was principally a fillings-supplier to the magor blending companies but over the last ten years, they have concentrated increasingly on marketing their own range of aged Malts and blends to the comsumer worldwide. In 1996, they bought over the firm of J&W Hardie, makers of the famous 'Antiquary' blend and this product now joins the Tomatin portfolio.

There were six wash and five spirit stills prior to the 1973 addition of 6 more of each. When production was cut back at the beginning of the 1980s, it was done by closing down the entire new set of stills. Such is technology today that one man can operate the entire distilling operation when all 23 stills are in action. With so many stills, there was a prodigious amount of waste hot water produced and Tomatin spent £100,000 on a commercial eel farm project. Elvers were raised in tanks and they grew as much in eight months in the balmy distillery run-off temperatures as would have taken two years in the cooler wild. Although markets were found the project

5

closed in 1984.

Tomatin's maltings were retained until 1973 before going over to central maltsters for supplies. Given the scale of operation, floor malting would have satisfied a tiny proportion of the modern production capacity at Tomatin.

The water source is the Allt na Frithe burn, a name that translates as the 'Freeburn'. A hotel of that name at Tomatin used to offer the privilege of fishing for salmon and trout in the nearby Findhorn to anyone registering as a resident for a few days.

The Whisky

Tomatin is elegant and airy with understated sweet, floral flavours and quite big smooth texture. It is available on the UK market as a 10 year old malt (soon to be upgraded to a 12 year old) and it is also used extensively in the company's 5 year old and 12 year old 'BIG T' Blended Whiskies. On the export market, Tomatin is increasingly enjoying growing sales, especially in the USA and Japan. The independents also offer 'Tomatin' in the bottle in limited quanitites from a variety of wood types and ages. Some 1970 vintages are still avaiable from specialist outlets.

Left: A crofter's cottage at the Culloden Moor museum gives an indication of the common form of housing in the area at the time of Bonnie Prince Charlie.

Of interest nearby

• **Cairngorm Whisky Centre** near Aviemore has just about everything to do with bottled whisky. Enormous range of miniatures stocked. Tastings held.
• **Loch Ness** is deep, dark and may indeed have a 'monster' other than occultist Aleister Crowley who lived by its shore. Be advised – don't scoff. Too many people,

locals and visitors, have seen something, many of the sightings not even published because they seem so impossible. BBC TV presenter Nicholas Witchell wrote a book on it all and in 1979 a BBC camera team shot 10 minutes of film of something moving fast through the water and leaving a substantial wake. Naturalist the late Sir Peter Scott came up with computer-enhanced pictures after a hi-tec investigation.

• **Culloden Moor** is where the final act of the Jacobite Rebellions took place in 1746. The clansmen were cut down by the Hanoverian forces and those not dead finished off with *coups de grâce* where they lay or crawled. Communal graves are scattered about the moor and woodland, the stumpy headstones indicating clan names only. There is an interpretative centre and museum on site.

•**Urquhart Castle** is a very picturesque ruin on the loch-shore below Drumnadrochit.

•**Castle Stuart**, ancient seat of the Royal House of Stuart family, the Earls of Moray, is visible on the Fort George road. The crown surmounting the round tower indicates the regal status of the family.

• The **Clava Cairns** are just down the road from Culloden, a trio of Palaeolithic chambered burial tombs with surrounding stone circles. Look out for the inscribed cup-and-ring marks, thought to be associated with magico- religious ritual.

Left: Castle Urquhart, positioned on a knoll overlooking Loch Ness, is one of the largest castles in Scotland. It was badly damaged in 1688, after King James VII fled into exile, and finally fell into decay the following year after a seige involving William of Orange's forces.

Trail 6 ❀ West Coast & Islands

From Campbeltown to Kyle of Lochalsh

Introduction

This is a long and complicated trail which, besides spanning three different whisky regions and 14 distilleries, traverses a part of Scotland that is rich and diverse in history as well as dramatic and lovely in scenery. In past times whisky and heather ale were made in tiny quantities for self-use on every island which supported populations. Proof of the antiquity of this activity emerged recently when archaeological excavation on the small island of Rhum produced a pottery shard containing solidified dregs of heather ale. Staff at the Glenfiddich laboratories brewed a fresh batch from analysis of the contents and were able to taste what prehistoric man drank 4000 years ago. How much longer was it, one wonders, before the next step – primitive, probably accidental, distillation – took place?

The trail starts in the Campbeltown whisky region before moving on to that of Islay. Under the initial loose four-region division of whisky-origin (see page 16), Jura, Mull and Skye were uncritically included in the Highland category but latterly an Islands sub-region (excluding Islay) which groups them together has come into use. Oban and Ben Nevis are West Highland malts.

Above: The west coast is punctuated with deep inlets, lochs and harbours, like this one on the Kintyre peninsula.

Springbank Distillery

Location: **Campbeltown, Argyll PA28 6ET**
Visitors welcome by appointment
Group bookings, max. 10 • No reception centre or shop
Tel: **01586-552085** *Fax:* **01586-553215**

*T*he family who own Springbank are direct descendants of the smugglers who originally made their illicit whisky on the very same spot. The distillery to this day is licensed to J. & A. Mitchell & Co. Ltd. and the present managing director is the great-great-great-grandson of the founder.

The ledger of a Campbeltown coppersmith from the early 1800s shows that Archibald Mitchell had a still but he never did anything about getting a licence. Although nothing shows in the official records until 1837, Springbank is thought to have been built on the site of the illicit operation in 1828 and the location seems to have been something of a 'Distillers' Row' since Longrow, Rieclachan, Union, Springside and Argyll distilleries were all immediately adjacent. The Springbank buildings in use today are still the original ones of 1828 but the expanded premises also take in the remaining vestiges of all these other distilleries.

The Mitchells were one of three or four distilling dynasties in Campbeltown and they were involved with many other distilleries around the town through members of the family.

The distillery survived the catastrophic loss of reputation suffered by Campbeltown whisky in the 1920s although the depression caused it to close in 1926 for seven years. Springbank has come to be keenly appreciated since the 1980s saw the surge of interest in single malt whiskies and it is a top-selling Scotch malt in the important Japanese market. When the Duke of Argyll launched his own brand of prestige, export scotch 15 years ago, it was Springbank malt whisky that went into the bottles.

Unusually, possibly uniquely, the whole process of whisky production by traditional methods is carried out at Springbank. The barley is malted, the peat is

6

Above: Barrels stacked up outside the Victorian buildings at Springbank.

cut by distillery staff, the malt is dried on a kilning floor and the matured whisky is bottled. Everywhere else in Scotland, some or all of these processes are carried out by specialist operators on behalf of distilleries. Glenfiddich is the only other distillery in Scotland where bottling is done *in situ*.

The malt dries fast at Springbank, thanks to blown air that both penetrates the beds of malt and allows more concentrated permeation of the grains by the peat-smoke. Springbank is, nonetheless, a light-to-medium peated whisky.

There are three stills and the way they are used has caused debate as to whether the spirit is, or isn't, triple-distilled. In fact, only a proportion of spirit is distilled three times and it seems to enhance both the mellowness and flavour of the final distillate. A naked flame (oil now, but coal until very recently) is part of the wash still's heating system and a rummager, dragged round inside, prevents yeast from sticking and burning. It does, however, allow a degree of toasting which contributes to the final Springbank flavour. A bell on top of the rummager rings as it turns; if the ringing stops, something has gone wrong and the stillman knows to investigate. All the water comes from Crosshill Loch a mile away.

The Whisky

Words used to describe Springbank's flavours and aromas include smoky, woody, pronounced, round, complex and peaty; also sweet, iodine-fragrant, salty and fresh. Finish is seen as rich, creamy, delicate, classy, balanced, and smooth.

The 'standard' Springbank is 15-year-old and is widely available; 21, 25 and 30-year-old are also bottled by the distillery, all at 46% vol. Other ages and vintages going back to the 1960s are available from independents. On the more offbeat side, a recent batch of fully matured Springbank whisky turned out green (i.e. grass-coloured) after having been accidentally aged in an ex-rum cask. The Japanese snapped it up. And a one-off distillation of green (i.e. ecologically correct) whisky for a Welsh organic barley farmer may lead to the production of organic whisky.

A second malt whisky is produced at Springbank called Longrow, the name of one of the old neighbouring distilleries which closed almost a century ago. Malt is dried entirely by peat-smoke and giving an intense, smoky, medicinal, character. The idea of two differently styled malts from a single distillery was also implemented at Lagavulin and Glenburgie. Both 16 and a 17-year-old bottlings of Longrow at 46% vol are obtainable.

6

Glen Scotia Distillery

Location: **Campbeltown, Argyll**
Roads: **High Street**
Please telephone for visit details
Reception centre
Tel: **01586-552288**

Glen Scotia has been silent on frequent occasions this century, including a recent spell in the 1980s. However, the distillery keeps on bouncing back and welcomes visitors with its new facilities. The distillery had a very stable existence throughout the last century. From 1832 to 1895 it belonged to the original licensees, but then changed hands twice more before falling silent, as did so many of its neighbours, in the 1920s. For a while it belonged to the owners of Scapa distillery in Orkney, right at the other end of the country. It was owned by Gibson International, until 1994

6

when production again ceased. The new owners are Loch Lomond Distillery Co. Ltd. The buildings, including the malt barns and the barley lofts, are Victorian and the stillhouse is thought to be original. At some stage expansion took in a row of shops so that the yard now abutts the street. Glen Scotia maintained its cooperage function and there has always been a cooper on the distillery payroll and there is a small range of cask-making tools on display.

A single pair of stills contrasts with the set of three used at Springbank. The water is drawn from Crosshill Loch and the distillery's own wells which are 80 feet deep.

The distillery has a resident ghost, that of a previous owner, Duncan MacCallum, who committed suicide in 1930 after losing a fortune in a crooked business deal. He drowned himself in Campbeltown Loch, later made famous in a popular song by Scots entertainer, Andy Stewart. The singer dreams that the loch is full of whisky, not water, and tries to drink it dry.

The Whisky

Glen Scotia has 2000 casks in store which are maturing for bottling as a single malt at fourteen years of age at 40% vol. An independently bottled plain-cask 1979 vintage at 58% vol. is soft and sweet.

Generally, Glen Scotia is a lightly smoky, salty malt with a quite concentrated nose and good length despite a delicate structure.

Above: At the southern tip of the Kintyre peninsula, the Mull Lighthouse stands over the North Channel between Scotland and Northern Ireland.

*Left: Robert Louis
Stevenson's family had
business links with this part of
Scotland. This portrait, by
John Singer Sargent, is a
detail from a portrait now in
New York.*

Of interest nearby

• The **Crucifixion Painting** in a cave on Davaar Island dates from 1887. It was
painted in secret but is now seen by many visitors. The artist, aged 80, returned in
1934 to restore the painting and it is now regularly retouched by a local artist.
Access is by a tidal causeway – so check the flow-times before you go!

• **St. Kieran's Cave**, 25 feet above the highwater mark near Achinoan Head, is
thought to have been the earliest Christian chapel in Scotland.

• The **Lighthouse** at South Point on the Mull was built in 1788 and remodelled by
Robert Stevenson, lighthouse-engineer grandfather of *Treasure Island* author Robert
Louis Stevenson.

• Traces of **Former Distilleries** can still be seen in Campbeltown. When they
closed, the roofs were taken off to avoid incurring taxes and many became
warehouses to the surviving distilleries, such as Hazelburn for DCL. Benmhor still
had its pagoda head in place long after it closed and Longrow used to be where
Springbank now has its carpark.

6

Island of Islay

Islay is the southernmost of the whisky-producing islands of the Inner Hebrides. It lies to the west of the Kintyre peninsula. There are both Celtic and Norse strains to Islay's history and in the 12th century Somerled, King of Argyll, made Islay his capital, founded the Clan Macdonald and set up the rule of the Lords of the Isles which lasted for 300 years.

The island has fine sheep and cattle pasture and the fertile soil yields fine barley. The landscape is padded with many peat-bogs and the cuttings from them have provided life-giving heat to the islanders over long centuries. It is completely odourless in its natural state, but, when burned, it has a rich and pungent smell. Peat is a community asset on Islay and local inhabitants are permitted to dig their own as a fuel supply from certain mosses for a nominal payment of £10 a year.

The incidence of peat and the proximity of the distilleries to the sea are the main circumstances that make Islay a category in its own right in the classification of Scotch whisky. Peat and salty seaspray impart the bold aroma and flavour that are the prevailing keynotes which typify the category. Peat saturates the fine, soft water used for distillation and smoky heat dries the malted barley. Salt and seashore aromas are absorbed by the moist air that surrounds the casks of maturing spirit. Small wonder, then, that such influences show through generously in the whisky.

Other islands had their distilleries which vanished when it became easier to take supplies from outside the community, but not so on Islay. Its makes are so powerful and individual that they just couldn't be let go. Islay malts are the heart, the core, the engine-room (with Rolls Royce machinery, of course) of most Scotch blends and the full-throated single malts are widely favoured.

Malt whisky is the original, ubiquitous Scotch whisky and Islay malts were always in demand. However, a shift to blends of malt and grain whiskies signalled consumer interest in lighter products. From the tail-end of the 19th century, Islay was more in demand as a blending component than as individual self whiskies.

The relative isolation of Islay has meant the retention of many traditional routines and equipment. Three of the few hand-turned malting floors left in Scottish distilleries are to be found on Islay at Bowmore, Laphroaig and Ardbeg, although the latter is now closed and for sale.

Laphroaig Distillery

Location: **Port Ellen, Isle of Islay PA42 7DU**
Roads: **On A846 east of Port Ellen**
Seasons: **September – June, tours 10.30am & 2pm Mon – Fri; all visits by appointment •** *Tel:* **01496-302418**

*L*aphroaig is arguably the distinctive Islay malt, a pungent, primal, classy spirit that has come to embody not only the traditional style associated with the island but also the smell and earthy impact that the rest of the world regards as the essential persona of Scotch malt whisky. Before single malts were properly marketed in bottles, it was Laphroaig that the pundits had in mind when they said that consumers could not cope with such a thrusting, uncompromising whisky, and that they would have to be weaned on to it via the gentle Obans and Dalwhinnies of the world. How wrong they were!

The Johnston family were farmers and distillers on Islay and John Johnston, who founded Laphroaig around 1812, while his brother ran the neighbouring Malt Mill distillery (the forerunner of Lagavulin) from 1816. In a gruesome accident in 1847, Donald, son of founder John, drowned (or was scalded to death) when he fell into a vat of burned ale, the boiled-up lees left behind after the first distillation in whisky making.

In 1837 yet another distillery was established immediately next door on the same coastal stretch. It was called Ardenistiel or Kildalton and two of the brothers Stein, a well-known distilling family in central Scotland, were brought in to run it. A third brother, Robert, had invented the first successful continuous still just 10 years before. Ardenistiel was later incorporated into Laphroaig when it failed, largely due to the neglect of the manager who was more interested in using the kilns to produce smoked ham during the distillery's silent season. He installed 2,000 pigs to graze on Texa islet just offshore from the distillery but that venture, too, failed and he went bankrupt.

6

In 1908 two Johnston sisters inherited and when they died in 1926 it was left to Ian Hunter, Isabella's son.

In a staff photograph taken in 1934, a secretary called Bessie Williamson, actually a Glasgow chemistry graduate, is seen standing beside a Laphroaig cask. She became company secretary and in 1954 the business was left to her. She was not the first lady-distiller in Scotland but at that particular time she was believed to be the only one; Bessie went on to become a respected and important figure in the Scotch whisky industry. She retired as managing director in 1972 and went to live in Ardenistiel House.

Laphroaig has its own peat source on a bog near Port Ellen airfield. The peat is cut and stacked each April, collected in August for storing and drying before being used during the following distillation season. The pair of stills installed in 1882 was augmented with a second pair – exact replicas – in 1923, two more in 1968 and then a single additional spirit still, making seven in all, in 1974. The lyne-arms at the top of the stills rise just above the horizontal in conducting the distillation vapours towards the condensers. When a new distillery boiler was ordered in 1955, it was delivered by being floated from the transport ship to the shore.

Laphroaig still operates its floor maltings, a rarity nowadays in the rest of Scotland, but a feature of Bowmore and Laphroaig distilleries. The barley is steeped for two days then spread out on the maltings floor for seven days, where it is hand-turned every eight hours using flat wooden shovels called shiels.

Part of Laphroaig's particularity is its medicinal aroma – first-time tasters are often reminded of iodine, cough mixture or disinfectant – and this helped it sell in the US during Prohibition – to the extent even of being made available on medical prescription.

Above: When Laphroaig distillery was first built, the small fishing town of Port Ellen provided a route for distributing the spirit.

The Whisky

Laphroaig is normally available at 10 and 15 years old, at 40% and 43% vol.

Recent bottlings include 10 year old cask strength at 57.3% and a 18 year old called Vintage 1977. This, and a 20 year old called Vintage 1976 are available only through duty free outlets and at the distillery.

A 30 year old Laphroaig has just been made available for 1977 release.

6

Lagavulin Distillery

Location: **Port Ellen, Isle of Islay PA42 7DZ**
Roads: **On A846 at Dunyveg**
Seasons: **All year, all visits by appointment • *Tel:* 01496-302250**

Lagavulin is one of the great whiskies of Scotland, a grand and complex spirit that epitomises the richly peaty style that is traditionally associated with Islay. It is produced on the Kildalton shore in the south-east of the island with Port Ellen just to the west.

Perhaps the first documented record of Lagavulin was when the folk-hero Scottish king, Robert the Bruce, fled here after defeat in battle against the Earl of Pembroke. Further testimony to tempestuous times is the ruin of Dunyveg Castle which still stands guard over Lagavulin Bay; in the 14th century it was a stronghold of the Lords of the Isles. In Gaelic Dun-naomhaig (Dunyveg – mh is pronounced v in Scots Gaelic) means 'fort of the little ships', referring to the fact that the castle had a sea-gate as well as an entrance on the land side. The Lords' vessels could be drawn up for repair inside the safety of the walls.

The distillery lies below the Dunyveg promontory and covers about six acres on Lagavulin Bay. It is the sole surviving unit of a bustling illicit distillation complex that spread along the foreshore in the 1740s. There were almost a dozen bothies - small primitive distillation shelters - ranged alongside a mill in a little hollow in the ground, the laggan mhouillin of the whisky's name. By 1817 there were just two distilleries on the site and by the 1830s only one remained.

6

Above: Traditional wooden fermentation vessels – on a grand scale – are in use at Lagavulin.

In 1867 the distillery was bought by the company of Peter Mackie, a dynamo of a man who had studied distillation techniques at Lagavulin. He went on to create the White Horse Scotch brand and used Lagavulin malt whisky as its heart – which is still the case today. Mackie was later knighted for his business achievements. Over the decades, buildings were added and by the end of the century the distillery was an interesting patchwork of architecture from several different periods. At that time few distilleries sold their whisky as unblended single malts; Lagavulin did so, however, and the product was very highly regarded. It sold in Glasgow, England and the colonies.

One of his whisky projects at the distillery was Malt Mill – an effort to produce an authentic, traditional 'old-fashioned' malt whisky differently from that yielded by the 'advanced' technology of his day. In effect he was trying to maintain the character and high quality of the old smugglers' whiskies. Even in those days, there were feelings that the product was being altered by the volume-production techniques being used in distillation. Malt Mill was a separate distillery set up on the same site in 1908. It was small-scale, used only peat – no coal – to dry the malt and the whisky was completely different in style from that of Lagavulin itself. Production stopped in 1960 but the Malt Mill stills were used for a while in the production of Lagavulin before being replaced. The distillery's visitor centre is the old Malt Mill Maltings.

The twin pagoda heads are still in place, lending that distinctive and vaguely mysterious quality to distillery exteriors. The pair of large grinding stones in position outside the distillery were used in the Malt Mill operation. The pier is a reminder of the attractive little 'puffers' that used to ply between the distillery and Glasgow, transporting barley, coal and casks, in the first half of the century.

The island distilleries that belonged to United Distillers had their own puffer for a while, a famous craft called the SS Pibroch. It acquired the nickname of the 'Fleetwood Lifeboat' in 1937 when it rescued crewmen from a trawler based in the port, which had foundered on the rocks off the Scottish islands. During the months that followed, the Pibroch crew were overwhelmed with boxes of fish gratefully pressed upon them by passing trawlers. During the war, a German U-boat surfaced near the Pibroch and an officer scrutinised it through binoculars from the conning tower. The submarine did not intervene but the officer might well have considered a boarding party had he known the Pibroch was Glasgow-bound with a cargo of Lagavulin whisky. Before the pier was built, full casks of spirit used to be floated out to the boats at anchor. Roll-on-roll-off ferries now enable road-lorries to transport all supplies to and from the distillery.

Part, at least, of Lagavulin spirit's individuality comes from the unique shape of the two pairs of stills, which are noticeably broad-necked. Also, the lead-off pipes (the lyne-arms) from the tops of the stills are more steeply angled than those in other distilleries. Water is brought down to Lagavulin from the two Solan lochs on the hillside above.

Above: Enjoying a 'wee dram' in the evening mists across the bay from Lagavulin.

The Whisky

Lagavulin has the same broad Islay characteristics as Laphroaig – weight, impact, power, concentration – but the details are different. There is a sweet'n'spicy dash to the malt, and a definite elegance that helpfully keeps the complexity in hand. Until recently Lagavulin was bottled at 12 years and 43% vol. but this stretched to 16 years when it became part of the company's Classic Malts range. There is also a 14-year-old from an independent and one of the specialist chains in the UK.

Bowmore Distillery

Location: School Street, Bowmore, Isle of Islay PA43 7GS
Daily guided tours: Mon-Fri 10.30am and 2pm
Summer: 11.30am and 3pm, Sat: 10.30am.
Party bookings by appointment • Admission charges
Reception centre, shop and video show.
Tel: **01496-810441**

---

*T*he town of Bowmore was 'moved' from what is now Bridgend in the late 1760s. It was the decision of the local laird, Daniel Campbell, and such relocations were almost a family trait; the Duke of Argyll, Clan Campbell Chief, had already done the same thing with Inveraray village on Loch Fyne on the mainland, moving the smells and noise of the hoi polloi from beneath the windows of his fine castle.

Bowmore's church, built in 1769, was circular in shape so as to deny the Devil corners in which to hide while he tried to tempt the congregation. It stood atop the hill outside the town and apart from it; the distillery was built at the bottom of the hill, snug within the town. Today the main street climbs up the hill to the church's doors, the expanded town lying beyond the pavements on both sides.

The distillery was built in 1779, making it one of the oldest in Scotland. In those days whisky making was carried out all over the island, each bothy-operator aiming to supply himself and sell some on to local clientele. There was plenty such activity around Bowmore, since the town offered a relatively high density of population, and although most of this production was illicit, it tended to be very good.

Bowmore's founder, David Simson, farmed and distilled at Bridgend and moved

6

Above: The distillery at Bowmore nestles on the shore. In the foreground is the famous Round Church.
Left: The filled casks have to be checked regularly to ensure there are no 'leakers'.

to Bowmore with the town. He was something of an entrepreneur, owning the little supply vessel that served the island, so no doubt some of his whisky penetrated to the far-off urbanity of Glasgow on the mainland. The Simson family sold out in 1837 to the Mutters, of whom James was the Ottoman, Portuguese and Brazilian vice-consul in Glasgow and also had farming interests on the island. Islay has lush, fertile soil and, as well as cropping wheat and, appropriately, barley, Mutter introduced clover to the island for use as animal fodder. When the distillery was expanded an aqueduct channelled more water from the River Laggan.

6

The family sold the distillery in 1892 and there was a succession of owners over the next 50 years or so. One of Bowmore's grain lofts was used during the last war as a Coastal Command operations room to monitor and control great Sunderland and Catalina flying boats, which flew countless U-boat-spotting sorties into the Atlantic. In 1963, whisky-brokers, Stanley P. Morrison Ltd., bought the distillery and have developed the whisky into a high-profile international brand which has continuously won top awards in international tasting competitions. Bowmore whisky was bought for despatch to Windsor Castle on behalf of Queen Victoria on more than one occasion and, while the appropriate invoice may have been issued, the monarch was required to pay no duty; a principle with which the smugglers of Islay and elsewhere had long agreed.

The pagoda heads show attractive individuality. The crests are onion-shaped like transplants from the Kremlin in Moscow and, taken together with the flat-brimmed eaves, look like the hats worn by Canadian Mounties. The stillhouse holds four copper stills and many of the other large vessels in the distillery are also made of copper – unusual in today's distilleries where stainless steel has made great inroads to wood and cast iron. Also very rare are Bowmore's three floor maltings and kiln which are still in use. No fuel is used for the kilning process for which blowers push air through the malt from radiators heated by waste water from the distilling process. Precise amounts of peat are burned only to impart the required degree of aroma and flavour. The original storage cellars at Bowmore go underground and contain a cask of 1981 vintage that was presented to the present Queen on her visit there. It's maturing nicely for now.   General Manager James MacEwan could be described as the all-round whisky man; in his time he has also been a cooper and a whisky-blender. Very much a part of the community, the distillery also uses that waste hot water from the distillation process to heat the island's swimming pool in one of the warehouses that was gifted by Bowmore Distillery to the townspeople.

6

The Whisky

Bowmore is a classic Islay malt that has a lighter persona but retaining a beautiful balance of peat with good, firm iodine-and-seashore complexity. It has great floral finesse and has been increasing in popularity in recent years. Bowmore is generous in the different ages and strengths at which it is released, with Bowmore Legend 12, 17, 21 and 25-year-old as well as 22 and 30 year old ceramics.

Above: Bowmore's four stills can be viewed from the visitors' gallery.
Left: The tun room has recently been refurbished. The vessels are made of Oregon pine.

Bruichladdich Distillery

Location: **Bruichladdich, Isle of Islay PA49 7UN**
Road: **A847 from Bridgend**
Closed. No visitors

*B*ruichladdich lies directly across Loch Indaal from Bowmore but, unlike it, can be plainly seen on its shore-road site. To the south is Port Charlotte which used to have its own distilleries. Octomore went out of business in 1852, although its dilapidated buildings can still be seen; Lochindaal was dismantled in 1929 and taken over by the Islay Creamery. Now Bruichladdich is the only distillery on the entire peninsula, and, the object of a takeover by the Whyte & Mackay Group (part of the American Brands corp) has been mothballed since March 1995.

The distillery was built in 1881 at a time when there was growing popularity worldwide of blended Scotch. The Harvey family of Glasgow were already distillers and they remained as owners, then important shareholders right through to 1929 when Bruichladdich stopped production. In 1938 it was one of a number of Scottish distilleries that was bought by a group of North Americans anxious to cater for the post-Prohibition market in the US.

The two remaining members of staff hope that it will be reopened one day. But the whisky will be around for some years yet.

The Whisky

Bruichladdich is light and whispery although it delivers good flavour and aroma. It is normally bottled at 10 years old and 40% or 43% vol. When older, it develops greater richness, sweetness and spiciness, though not always in the typical Islay manner. There are 15- and 21-year-olds as well as 25-year-old Stillman's Dram. Independents do 19-, 23- and 25-year-olds at about 46% vol.

Caol Ila Distillery

Location: **Port Askaig, Isle of Islay PA46 7RL**
Roads: **Access from the A846**
Seasons: **All year. All visits by appointment • *Tel:* 01496-840207**

Caol Ila is not a pretty distillery by any stretch of the imagination, but the view outwards from it is exhilarating. The buildings are tucked in the lee of a hill on the seashore by the ferry from Jura and you look over to the famous Paps of Jura rearing on the far hinterland. The still house is glass-fronted and these shapely mountains are always in view as the still house staff go about their daily work. The ferry was the crossing-point for the Islay cattle-drovers, today's tranquillity such a contrast to the bellowing of the herds and the drunken shouting of the herdsmen that must have filled the air when a drove was on.

Caol Ila dates from 1846 and was built at this lovely but remote spot by Hector Henderson who had business connections with Littlemill (Lowlands) and some now long-defunct Campbeltown distilleries. He went on to invest in two other distilleries – Lochindaal on Islay and Camlachie in Glasgow – but he overstretched himself and had to sell up in 1852. It was bought by the owner of Isle of Jura distillery but he too had to find a buyer just a decade later – Bulloch Lade and Co. who were Glasgow blenders. This was the beginning of Caol Ila's subsequent reputation as a top blending malt.

Bulloch Lade rebuilt the distillery in 1879, making use, in the process, of a newly patented substance called concrete; it was the first building on Islay to do so. Caol Ila continued to produce up to the present day with short periods of closure from 1930 to 1937 (under new owners DCL) and during World War II. The distillery was again rebuilt in 1972 as the stark functional structure that makes you wince when you first glimpse it from the ferry.

Caol Ila – simply Gaelic for the Sound of Islay on whose shore it stands – used to be on the delivery route of DCL's famous puffer coaster, the SS Pibroch. It was still working the west coast recently, although this was for other owners since it was sold in 1972. There are six stills, four of them dating from the 1972/4 rebuilding. Some of the casks of spirit from Caol Ila are matured in the warehouses of the old Lochindaal distillery near Port Charlotte, which was closed in 1929.

Above left: In the mid-19th century, the owner of Caol Ila also had two other distilleries. Camlachie, in Glasgow, had a finely engraved label. Above right: The view out from the still house at Caol Ila is particularly dramatic.

The Whisky

Caol Ila has the pepper, smoke and peat of Islay but it has its own velvety, oily/glycerine texture and middleweight presence. It has only recently become available as a bottled malt but even now its distribution is very limited. It is certainly available at the distillery, but is just as likely to be encountered in Italy, where they are great Scotch malt *cognoscenti*, as in high streets around Britain. Standard issue is 15 years old at 43% vol., but there have recently been 12- and 13-year-olds at different strengths as well as 1978 and 1972 vintages from independents.

6

Bunnahabhain Distillery

Location: **Port Askaig, Isle of Islay PA46 7RP**
Seasons: **All year** • *Hours:* **10am - 4pm Mon - Fri**
All visits by appointment • **Group bookings max 12**
Reception centre and shop • *Tel:* **01496-840646**

*T*he sleeve of water that separates Islay from Jura to the east begins to widen out where the little distilling outpost of Bunnahabhain sits on the shore. The boat you see apparently waiting to unload malt has, in fact, been there since 1974 when it was cast on to the rocks. The distillery sits mainly to one side of the pier and climbs the hillside part of the way. Houses on harbour front and hillside take up the other side of the pier and sheep wander everywhere just as cats do in mainland suburbs.

There was a time when tourists bought Bunnahabhain ('Boon-a-havn') for all the wrong reasons. Funny, unpronounceable names often attract attention but this one also happens to be the top-selling brand, malt or blend, at the Scotch Whisky Heritage Centre in Edinburgh. It is one of Islay's gentle malts and quietly enjoying its status as a malt to be 'discovered'. Bunnahabhain features in the Famous Grouse Scotch blend which is owned by the distillery's proprietors.

Bunnahabhain was established in 1881 – the same year as Bruichladdich – and for the same reason – to meet the growing demand for whisky for the blending industry – but materialised at the isolated opposite end of the island, beyond even remote Caol Ila. This was probably because blending company Robertson & Baxter

Right: A cooper at work, renovating barrels ready for the maturation process at Bunnahabhain.

particularly liked Caol Ila's whisky and set out to produce their own in the same style by building close by. The proprietors even had to build their own road just to get things started; houses and food-stores for the distillery workers and a school for their children followed. Bunnahabhain became a fine example of the self-sufficient distilling communities that had grown up all over Scotland. Alfred Barnard, who toured Scottish distilleries in the 1880s, described Bunnahabhain, as a 'life-like and civilised colony'. The name means 'river-mouth', referring to the River Margadale alongside.

The malt whiskies produced on Islay are generally thought to be peaty, pungent and seaweedy. But since 1883 Bunnahabhain has been creating a fine mellow whisky that is one of the smoothest and subtlest of the island's malts.

Just a few years after its construction, Bunnahabhain's owners joined up with two other distilling firms to form Highland Distilleries and to this day they remain the proprietors. The distillery closed for a short period in the early 1980s but has since reopened, its production apparently secure at least for the present. With a name the length of 'Bunnahabhain Distillery' it would not be surprising if the two warehouses at the water's edge which bear the words were deliberately built long enough to carry all the letters. A single pair of stills was augmented by a second pair in 1963.

"Westering Home"...

Bunnahabhain
SINGLE ISLAY MALT SCOTCH WHISKY
PRODUCT OF SCOTLAND
THE BUNNAHABHAIN DISTILLERY COMPANY,
BUNNAHABHAIN, ISLE OF ISLAY, SCOTLAND, BOTTLED IN SCOTLAND

The Whisky

Bunnahabhain is a soft, light malt at least partly due to the natural lack of peat in the water and light peating. This change from the heavily peaty style of the past has come about by the distillery's trapping spring water in the hills to avoid its running through the peat-beds. The whisky tends also to show floral and fruity tones, everything coming over with considerable subtlety. The 'middle cut' of each distillation run is said to be particularly small and a proportion of sherry casks is used for maturing the spirit. Twelve years and 40% or 43% vol. is customary and variations from independents are few and far between, though vintages from 1982 and 1979 at high strengths have cropped up recently.

Of interest on Islay

• The **Parliament** of the 14th-century independent Gaelic principality run by the Lords of the Isles was located in the stronghold on the island in Loch Finlaggan. New chiefs were proclaimed from there and treaties with foreign governments against the Scottish crown were ratified there. There are several carved stones on the island.

• The **Museum of Islay Life** at Port Charlotte gives a good perspective on the islanders' lifestyles over the centuries in their main occupations of farming, fishing and distilling. Among the exhibits is an illicit still that was used in the hills nearby over a long period of time.

• The **Cross of Kildalton** is eighth-century Celtic, yet in fine condition. There was much activity in these parts in establishing Christianity; Iona, place of pilgrimage where St. Columba is thought to have first landed, is close by.

• The **Oa Peninsula**, which makes up the south-western section of the island, was used by smugglers due to the large number of caves there. Spectacular cliffscapes give it a wild aspect with views in all directions.

• Have a dip in the **Bowmore Distillery Swimming Pool**, heated by waste-waters from the distillation runs.

Left: From Port Askaig on the sound of Islay it is only a very short distance to the Isle of Jura.

Isle of Jura

Jura has long been a sparsely inhabited island. When local estate-owners commissioned the reconstruction of the old distillery at Craighouse in the early 1960s to try and revive the community, the 250-strong workforce brought in more than doubled the island's population. A single highway, the Long Road, runs round the southern and eastern sides of Jura and peters out towards the northernmost point, just past where novelist George Orwell wrote *1984*. The west coast is uninhabited. The island is not inhospitable, just undeveloped. Over 5,000 deer roam, mainly in the north, and gave the island its name (Jura derives from the Norse for 'Deer Island'). A long time ago there were also wild boar and the occasional wolf.

Half a dozen crofts are worked on Jura today but in the past there were many more – and cottars too. The latter had no land-entitlement, working for the laird and living in a tied cottage. Cottars had to do stipulated duty-work without payment and if they did not maintain their houses well enough – including new thatch to the roofs every second year – they had to reimburse the laird for the fall in their value. If a cottar was visited by friends or family, two shillings per day had to be paid to the laird – the equivalent of a day's work. They even had to keep their pigs locked up until the potato crop was dug and their chickens cooped up during seeding and harvest time.

Jura seems to have escaped the abuses of the infamous Highland Clearances when tenants on estates were evicted to make way for sheep grazing. Many families did, however, surrender to the lure of emigration to try for a better life in the colonies. Jura was part of the drovers' route to mainland cattle trysts and the drove roads ran across the south of the island from the ferry at Feolin to Lagg on the east coast.

The conventions of Highland hospitality required that travellers be taken in, fed and given shelter for the night. However, this often caused hardship for many country-dwellers who were extremely poor, so change-houses – wayside inns – were introduced to remove the burden. The Long Road had four or five change-houses.

Jura is part of the Highland category of malt whiskies although recent attempts to lend greater precision to classifying styles place it in an Island sub-group (see page 16).

Above: The Paps of Jura with the car ferry from Kintyre to Islay in the foreground.

Isle of Jura Distillery

Location: **Craighouse, Isle of Jura PA60 7XT**
Seasons: **September - May, 9am - 4pm Mon - Fri; all visits by
appointment • *Tel:* 01496-820240**

There is not much more to Craighouse in the south-east of the island of Jura than
the hotel and the distillery. It is a delightful little harbour with tufted, rocky islets
scattered about Small Isles Bay and looks pretty as a picture when the water reflects
moored yachts and the bright blue sky of a summer's day. The Paps rise in a cluster
to the north behind the Jura Forest and palm trees – the climate is very mild – rustle
in the breeze.

Isle of Jura is the only distillery on the island and may well have been the only
legal one; part-timers supplemented its supply prior to the 19th century. Open-air
or cave-based illicit production around Craighouse is thought to have progressed to
distillation in buildings in the village by 1810; certainly the local laird had a mill
with kilning facilities built at Craighouse in 1775, which would have been useful for
preparing malt. It was a time of expansion for Jura. Two years later, Thomas Telford
completed the new road round the south of the island and there were change-houses
at Feolin Ferry from Islay, Craighouse, Corran House, Lagg Ferry to Keills on the
mainland and Kenuachdrach in the north.

The first post office opened at Lagg and the mail for Islay went by runner to Port
Askaig and a second runner took it down to Bowmore. It was not until 1831 that
William Abercrombie was listed as the distillery's first licensee although until 1876
there was a number of operators, only two of whom lasted more than 12 months or
so. In that year James Ferguson bought the business and rebuilt the distillery. The
conditions of his lease from the local laird were very demanding and eventually
friction and illwill prompted the Ferguson family to strip out their stills and
machinery and abandon the distillery in 1901. Almost 20 years later, the Fergusons
were still being pursued in court for payment of repairs the laird insisted was due.
The roofs were taken off to avoid having to pay rates on the buildings and the shells

Above: Craighouse has a small jetty, which today is mainly used by small pleasure craft.

remained thus until 1960, when a new distillery began to take shape thanks to two local men.

George Orwell's landlord and the owner of the Jura estate commissioned the rebuilding of the distillery to help stimulate the local economy. Jura's original production yielded a heavy, peaty whisky in the style of Islay just across the Sound, but when the new distillery was completed in 1963 the architect designed the whisky as well as the buildings. William Delmé-Evans aimed at the wider appeal of a lightly peated Highland malt and prescribed the tall stills needed to do the job. The distillery is now owned by the Whyte & Mackay group.

The whitewashed buildings sit pertly on the rise from the harbour, the cooperage from the original still in place at the edge of the roadway. The Jura Hotel opposite in an earlier guise was one of Jura's change-houses going back to 1742 and before; the lounge bar today used to be a thatched 'room and kitchen'. The view to the Small Isles and beyond is unimpeded.

The 1963 pair of stills was augmented by a second pair in 1978, all four being larger than most – a circumstance that contributes to the lightness of the whisky. In the same year building materials were transported by helicopter up to the water source, Market Loch, to construct a dam. The distillery has two separate water-systems: that direct from the loch is used for whisky making, and the 'town' water, which is sometimes chlorine-fragrant, for everything else. The spirit-receiver was made in the distinctly non-whisky-making town of Jarnac, at the heart of France's Cognac country!

The Whisky

As touched on above, up to the turn of the century the whisky made at Jura was big and peaty like those of neighbouring Islay, but when the distillery was reborn in 1963, the stills were designed to produce the lighter, distinctly Highland-style of whisky now associated with the island name. Its lightness shows in its silky gentleness, but it still has excellent presence with subtly peaty flavour, mellowness and balance. It is bottled at 10 years and at two strengths, 40% and 43% vol. Bottlings from individual casks through the independents are rare but a 1972 is available from one of the societies and Jura also produces its own special edition, the Stillman's Dram, which is currently a 26-year-old.

Left: The Paps of Jura rise steeply from the horizon, and are the site of an annual Fell Race each May, sponsored by the distillery.

Of interest on Jura

• At **Craighouse** the 1775 mill stands opposite the distillery. It pre-dates even the earliest whisky-making buildings on the site but still has much of its machinery intact.

• At **Ardmenish** are the remains of another mill, and at **Torran Dubha**, near Ardlussa, the ruin of a kiln, both of which were associated with illicit distilling.

• At **Daimh-Sgeir**, south of Feolin, is the grave of Jura's very own highwaywoman who used to attack the mail-carriers from Islay. In the summary justice of the day, she is said to have been 'disposed of' by a local man in return for the gift of a farm. By the bridge near her grave is a gate-post from one of the numerous sets of gates that had to be negotiated in travelling on the Long Road.

• At **Barnhill**, near the northern end of the Long Road, George Orwell wrote his novel *1984* in the cottage there. It was completed in 1948 and he simply reversed the last two digits of the year for the book's title. Orwell liked a drink but preferred Lamb's Navy rum to whisky. It is not generally realised that the author had sold up in London and gone to live permanently on Jura. He died in 1950.

• **Kilearnadil**, a former township north-west of Craighouse, was wiped out by the plague and, beside the graveyard carpark, are the ruins of a house that was pulled down on top of the bodies of the last family to succumb to it. It is regarded as both tomb and memorial to those who died during the plague epidemic. Nearby, Jura Parish Church (built 1766) has a stone bench outside the door where the Gaelic-speaking parishioners would sit and wait until the English-speaking service was over. The service in their own language would then follow.

• The **Gulf of Corryvreckan** lies off the north coast between Jura and Scarba. The famous whirlpool is classified as un-navigable by the Royal Navy and is most spectacular between flood and half-flood tide. George Orwell was briefly marooned on the Eilean Mor islet when he sailed into the race and his boat fell apart; had it not been during a relatively quiescent phase, there might have been no such book as *1984* in the body of English literature today.

6

• Beside **Corran House**, one of the old change-houses, lies the island emergency airstrip which is maintained for the benefit of the island by Lord Astor, owner of one of the six estates into which Jura is divided.
• Volcanic action formed the Inner Hebridean islands like Jura and there are hundreds of **Lava Dykes** to be seen across its landscape, all of which orientate towards the island of Arran, souce of the eruption.
• Keep an eye open for golden eagles, wild goats and stags. The north-west has **caves** to explore, including one that was fortified; there are many prehistoric **forts** and **burial cairns**; there are raised beaches, formed when climatic changes caused the sea-levels to drop.

• M o v i n g   o n •

After Jura distillery, the trail may be continued either by ferry via the island of Colonsay to Oban, or by returning to Kennacraig. Between here and Oban, where the next distillery is located, of interest are:
• At **Inveraray**, the actual 19th-century jail and courthouse have live 'warders' and 'prisoners' as guides. Talk to them, visit the furnished cells, and sit in on the trials. Behave yourself, though, or you may be locked into one of the exercise cages!
• **Inveraray Castle**, splendid home of the Duke of Argyll, chief of the Clan Campbell, who has his own brand of whisky. Inveraray was the base where seaborne landing techniques evolved. Robert Adam was involved in redesigning the beautiful lochside town when it was moved from its old location in the 18th century.
• **Poltalloch** is a widely scattered prehistoric complex featuring an extraordinary concentration of neolithic chambered tombs, stone circles, standing stones and

Left: Inverary Castle houses a splendid arms collection and a combined operations warfare museum.

inscribed rocks near Kilmartin. Dunadd was an important Dark Age hill-fort.
• **Carnasserie** and **Kilchurn** castle ruins are substantial and in beautiful settings. Carnasserie is a fine 16th-century tower house burned in clan warfare; its staircase and wall-walk are still intact. Kilchurn has an overwhelmingly romantic setting on a peninsula on Loch Awe with a great sweep of mountains all around.
• The old **Iron Furnace** at Bonawe was set up nearly 250 years ago and is the most complete remaining charcoal-fired ironworks in Britain.

Oban Distillery

Location: **Oban, Argyllshire PA34 5NH**
Roads: **Just off esplanade below McCaig's Tower on hill**
Seasons: **All year, 9.30am - 5.00pm Mon - Fri; Easter - October**
Mon - Sat. Last tour 4.00pm • Group bookings by appointment
Reception centre and shop • *Tel:* 01631-564262

*T*he West Highland town of Oban lies in a very pretty position on the Firth of Lorn with the green islands of Lismore and Kerrera offshore and the bulk of Mull rising behind. The spot has long been appreciated as a safe anchorage and usually bristles with yacht masts; it is also the terminal for ferries to Mull and other islands. Oban's antiquity as a place of settlement is vividly expressed by its being the type-site in world archaeology of the Mesolithic Obanian culture. Worked stone implements, perhaps from as long ago as 4500 BC, were found here and indeed part of the discovery was made in a rock-shelter that was exposed during extension work in the Oban distillery yard. The Colosseum-like McCaig's Tower sits on a cliff above the town like a giant tiara. It is an excellent reference point for anyone seeking the distillery which lies immediately below.

Boswell and Johnson found a 'tolerable inn' when they visited Oban during their

Above: The sea front at Oban, with boat trips and pipers, is one of the tourist centres of the area.

1773 Highland jaunt; perhaps they were luckier than they realised, considering it was still no more than a fishing hamlet at the time. Sir Walter Scott passed through in 1814 and Mendelssohn in 1829 on his way to see Fingal's Cave on Staffa.

The distillery at Oban was founded in 1794 by the local Stevenson brothers who had been involved to some degree in the creation of the fishing port of Tobermory on Mull. The date makes Oban one of the oldest distilleries in Scotland, and it pre-dates the town which came to take shape around it. The first licence dates from 1797 but expired the following year despite a House of Commons report describing the distillery as one of the best equipped in the Highlands. For the next 20 years, the industrious Stevensons turned their attention to other matters. They were in the throes of developing Oban from the small fishing village it had been, and owned ship-building, slate-quarrying and house-building businesses.

The distillery was revived in 1818 and run by the Stevensons until the 1850s. A later owner rebuilt it in 1884, no doubt planning to capitalise on the faster transport to Glasgow and other large markets afforded by the railway, which had come to Oban town in 1880. It was during blasting operations in the cliff bounding the yard at the rear that a cave was revealed that had been used by Mesolithic settlers. Bones and stone tools were found, which are now in the National Antiquities Museum in Edinburgh. The site was sealed up following excavation. DCL bought the distillery in 1930 and had two periods of non-production – 1931 to 1937 and 1969 to 1972. During the latter closure the still house was rebuilt.

The distillery is set back from the harbour promenade in the heart of Oban town. The sea used to come right up to the door. What was originally the Stevensons' family house was eventually converted into offices. The sitting room had a peep-hole door which enabled checks to be made at any time on work in progress in the adjacent still house. At the start of World War II, the distillery men signed up to go to sea in the room that is now the manager's office; some of them were only 14 years old. The floor maltings closed in 1968 although it is still in place and listed as a historic building.

The still house was rebuilt in 1972 but the single pair of stills was not added to, although the heating method was converted from coal to steam. The stills are rather broad-necked in comparison to the longer, slimmer-necked stills seen in many other distilleries. Worm condensers are now quite rare in Scottish distilleries and the rectangular double worm-tub at Oban may well be unique. Oban's style is not over-robust but it is certainly long-lived. A Manchester merchant opened a bottle distilled at the end of the 19th century and reported the whisky as having a 'soft and fragrant nose'. Despite the belief that own-label whiskies are the creation of modern supermarket chains, the idea has long been in place in Scotland. Licensed grocers all over the country liked the *cachet* of having their very own brands and McKercher's of Oban sold single malt from the distillery under the Glenforsa brand name when it was hardly obtainable anywhere else.

The Whisky

Oban's house style is medium in body and flavour, slightly peaty and zesty, with smooth texture and finish. It used to be bottled at 12 years old, but the optimum age is now regarded as 14 years at 43% vol. by its owners who made it one of their range of six 'Classic Malts'. Independent firms have 1962, 1972 and 21-year-old editions at strengths varying from 40% to 46% vol. Greater dryness and peat come through in the older bottlings, with sweet-edge sherry overlay when aged in Jerez casks.

Left: The temperature of the wort has to be checked regularly.

Of interest nearby

• **McCaig's Tower** was commissioned in the 1890s as an act of philanthropy to keep local stonemasons in employment.

• **Dunollie Castle** is a 13th-century tower house with splendid views over the surrounding countryside. For this latter reason it was the main stronghold of the Scots Kings of Dalriada and later the Macdougalls, the Lords of Lorne. It was abandoned after the 1745 Jacobite Rebellion.

• **Dunstaffnage Castle** (13th century) was also originally a Macdougall castle. The Stone of Destiny was first brought here from Ireland. It was a ceremonial symbol of royal authority in the crowning of the Scottish Kings until Edward I of England, 'the Hammer of the Scots', removed it to Westminster Abbey as war-spoils. (In 1950 the

Above: Dunstaffnage castle has an attractive site in parkland close by the water's edge.

Stone briefly came back to Scotland when two Scottish Nationalists snatched it from beneath the Coronation Chair in the Abbey. It was restored months later.) After the Jacobites' defeat at the Battle of Culloden in 1746, Flora Macdonald spent 10 days at Dunstaffnage on her way to London as a prisoner of the English Crown.

• **The Oban Experience**, on Heritage Wharf, takes you back to the creation and development of the town as a port and railway terminus. You find out why Garibaldi, Wordsworth, Mendelssohn and Sir Walter Scott visited Oban.

• Ben Cruachan is Scotland's **Hollow Mountain** – it is stuffed with the machinery and pumps that create the hydro-electric power. Go inside and see for yourself.

• **Rare Breeds Farm Park** works with interesting variations on the usual breeds of sheep, pigs, cattle and poultry seen on farms.

• The **Scottish Salmon & Seafood Centre** is a working fish farm with interpretative exhibitions on the development of the Scotch salmon-farming industry and the life-cycle of salmon.

6

Isle of Mull

Mull's dramatic landscape has fluted, bare mountain flanks and volcanic cliffs contrasting with great sweeps of green glen and sheltered pastoral meadow. It wears its geology openly, so much of the land having been eroded over past millions of years, and it is also one of the best places in Scotland to see golden eagles, sea eagles and otters. It was the setting for R. L. Stevenson's novel *Kidnapped*.

Samuel Johnson liked his comforts and he considered Mull 'worse than Skye', but perhaps it was just a bad day for him when he visited Tobermory with Boswell because he had lost his fine oak walking stick. He certainly had a better time – 'the most agreeable Sunday I ever passed' – on the offshore isle of Inchkenneth with Sir Allan Maclean and his two daughters. Ulva Island is larger and was the birthplace of Lachlan Macquarrie, 'the Father of Australia', and earlier generations of the family of explorer/missionary David Livingstone.

Tobermory is an Island distillery in the broad Highland malt whisky category.

Top: A watery sunset over the Sound of Mull.
Above: The Isle of Mull is served by a regular ferry.

Tobermory Distillery

Location: **Tobermory, Isle of Mull**
Roads: **On the shore road at the edge of town**
Seasons: **Easter – end-October**
Hours: **10.00am – 5.00pm Mon – Fri.**
Group bookings max 12 • Reception centre and shop
Tel: **01688-302647**

There is a distinctly continental look to Tobermory on Mull. The blues, oranges and reds of the immaculate waterfront houses and the sentry-like residence on the wooded hill behind make it look more like Portofino than a Hebridean harbour. The town was briefly a centre of commerce in the late 18th century, and indeed was built expressly to be just that. The fine natural harbour made it the chosen site for a fishing station that was built from scratch, work beginning in 1788. Within four years both the fishing operation and general trade conducted through the port were substantial; it was only a matter of time (and a blind eye regarding planning permission) before a distillery became part of the scenery.

While there were certainly numerous stills in production over the centuries on Mull, Tobermory, or Ledaig as it was originally named, is the only permanent distillery to figure in official records. On Skye, today, there is only one remaining distillery – Talisker – and documents tell us the names, locations and a little history of the many that once were but are now no more. Not so on Mull. Tobermory seems to have been the island's sole legal distillery so it is pleasing that there are still those who see it as having a role to play in the island's life.

Among those involved in the creation of the town of Tobermory in 1788 were the Stevenson brothers of Oban who, just a few years later, went into whisky production in their own part of the world. In their case, however, it was the distillery that came first and the town of Oban that subsequently grew up around it. At Tobermory the application in 1797 by a merchant called John Sinclair to build a distillery was turned down because there were two other local stills already in operation. Sinclair declined the offer of permission to build a brewery instead, but when he reapplied the following year he was allowed to go ahead.

Sinclair was an energetic entrepreneur and did well enough from his several businesses to retire at the age of 43. He had built up an estate at Lochaline in Morvern to which he retired in 1825 when his wife died. His name remained on the licence until Ledaig closed down in 1837; Sinclair died in 1863 and his mansion at Lochaline is today a grass-grown ruin.

The distillery was revived in 1878, several owners coming and going before the distillery was closed for the long period 1930 - 1972. During the second world war it was used as a canteen for sailors stationed at a naval base at Tobermory. In 1972, it briefly fluttered into life again for three years but the new owners failed and a Yorkshire property firm came in. The present owners have not yet achieved uninterrupted production but the latest indications are that distillation will continue for the forseeable future. The water comes down to the distillery from the Mishnish Lochs. There are two pairs of stills.

The Whisky

Given the customary eight to 15 years' maturation afforded bottled single malt whiskies, any break in production becomes a problem for the future because the missing years restrict fine-tuning capabilities for the final product. Three years' missed distillation in, say, 10 do not just mean three years' lost sales; dearth of mid-term matured product for blending means that the whisky may well never be at its best at any time during that decade.

Above: Torosay Castle is a fine Victorian mansion near Tobermory.

At Tobermory they have made the best of their circumstances and are to be congratulated for doing so. The Tobermory name is used for both a malt and a blend. The malt is a vatted whisky, combining older Tobermory malt with malts from other distilleries, chosen for their broad similarity to Tobermory's own style. Single malt whisky from the distillery, which is usually from single years of production, can be obtained under the Ledaig label. Recently, 18 and 20-year-olds and a 1973 vintage have been on offer.

Of interest nearby

• The Florida, a **Spanish Galleon** from the Spanish Armada, sank in Tobermory Bay in 1588. A Maclean clansman, held prisoner on board, set fire to a magazine, effectively scuttling the ship. Tantalising items, including brass- and silverware, have been retrieved but the existence of rumoured treasure has yet to be proven.

• At Ardmeanach a **Fossil Tree** set into a cliff may be reached via a sometimes boggy but rewarding walk. There is also **Mackinnon's Cave**, very large and deep, the stone within thought to have been the altar of early Christian hermit-monks.

• The **Isle of Mull Wine Company** welcomes visitors to see its wine-making, blending and bottling operation at Bunessan.

• **Duart Castle** is the 13th-century home of the chiefs of the Clan Maclean. It sits on a clifftop, closely scrutinising every ferry that rounds this easternmost headland of Mull on its way to Craignure.

• **Torosay Castle** is a beautiful family home, designed and built by David Bryce, in 1858. It has 12 acres of gardens, formal and themed, and an Italian Statue Walk. It is possible to travel to it by a narrow gauge railway from Craignure, the only island passenger railway in Scotland. Visitors can see weavers working old dobby looms at their workshops in the grounds.

• Tiny **Staffa Island** to the west of Mull is the location of Fingal's Cave, made famous as part of the Hebrides Overture to Mendelssohn's Scotch Symphony. He visited the island, of course, as have numerous celebrities. Queen Victoria was rowed in aboard a barge; it must have been a very calm day because waves sloughing into the cave often jam driftwood into rock niches 20 feet above the water.

• **Iona**, off the south-west tip of Mull was the cradle of Scottish Christianity. It is the burial-place of Norse, Irish and early Scottish kings, including Duncan, murdered by Macbeth but perhaps not quite in the manner portrayed by Shakespeare. St. Oran's Chapel (1080) has a carved Norman door. St. Martin's Cross is ninth century, nearly 17 feet high and carved with runes.

Above: Iona abbey was founded by St Columba, who landed there in 563.

• Moving on •

• **Castle Stalker** is a most attractive 13th-century fortlet on its own islet just off the coast road from Oban to Fort William.

• **Glencoe** lies to the east, the moody, usually mist-wreathed, high-walled canyon where, in 1692, Robert Campbell of Glenlyon led a detachment of government soldiers in the slaughter of the MacIan Macdonalds, who had hosted them all for almost a fortnight, under the pretext that they had sworn allegiance to William III too late. The MacIans had actually signed the oath but were delayed in doing so.

Ben Nevis Distillery

Location: **Lochy Bridge, near Fort William PH33 6TJ**
Roads: **On A82 (Fort William-Inverness) near junction with A830 to Mallaig • *Seasons:* All year**
Hours: **9am – 5pm, Mon – Fri; also 10am – 4pm, Sat Easter – end-September • Group bookings max 15 per tour**
Reception centre, exhibition and shop • *Tel:* 01397-700200

*F*ort William was one of the 'forts and roads' network steadily built up in the Highlands by the London governments to control rebellious tendencies in the inhabitants. Most of the Highlanders were Jacobites and there was a succession of uprisings, those of 1715 and 1745 merely the best known. The town is dominated by the massive bulk of Ben Nevis, the highest mountain in Britain at just over 4000 feet.

'Long John' Macdonald was a very tall man and, although this fact was immaterial to the making of his whisky, the nickname eventually served well when it came to choosing a brand name. His distillery was founded in the shadow of Ben Nevis in 1825 and the 'Dew of Ben Nevis' was the first name given to his product. In fact his association with Ben Nevis was short – little over a year – but, with a succession of Macdonalds and Macdonells as licensees, it could be said to have at least remained within the clan. The distillery survived a sequestration in 1856 and the Long John name was sold in the 1920s, but in 1955 it was taken over by new owners with Joseph Hobbs as a moving force. Hobbs was an interesting character, a Scot who made a fortune in Canada and returned to Scotland and began buying whisky distilleries. Hobbs dabbled in new blending ideas, believing that whiskies would be greatly improved if 'married' – mixed together – for longer periods before bottling. No doubt he put some of his ideas into the Grand Reserve Blend that he had created for the splendid Inverlochy Castle Hotel which he owned nearby. The mansion was once Hobbs's home but is now one of Europe's top hotel/restaurants and still owned by his daughter-in-law.

Left: The snow stays on the peak of Ben Nevis into the early summer.

In 1878 a second distilling unit was built nearby as an extension to Ben Nevis itself. It was called Nevis and operated as a separate entity for 30 years before being absorbed into the Ben Nevis operation in 1908. A housing development occupies the site of Nevis distillery. Ben Nevis is now owned by the Japanese company, Nikka.

The water to make the whisky is drawn from the Allt a'Mhuilinn (the Mill Burn) that starts as snow-melt. It could hardly be purer or colder. The mash-tun is a Glenspey type lauter tun made of stainless steel. There are two pairs of stills today which date from the 1955 acquisition. A continuous still was also installed for making grain whisky, but is no longer on site.

The Whisky

A recent limited edition of 90 bottles from a 63-year-old cask of Ben Nevis whisky attracted prices as high as £2,000 a bottle. Dew of Ben Nevis is a blend. It is bottled at four and 12 years old, both 40% vol. The broad style is light in peat and sweetish with a grassy/spicy persona. Ben Nevis is a West Highland malt. Selections of malt whisky are bottled at cask strength and at various ages, in limited numbers.

Of interest nearby

• The **West Highland Museum** in Fort William is crammed with fascinating exhibits. There is the gun that killed the 'Red Fox' from Stevenson's *Kidnapped* and a shiny metal tube that transforms daubs of paint into a secret portrait of Bonnie Prince Charlie.
• **Glenfinnan Station** on the stunningly beautiful West Highland railway line has been made over to an interpretative centre and railway museum.
• The **Cable Cars** on Aonach Mor are the only ones of their type in Britain.
• **Roy Bridge** is the site of the last clan battle that took place in Scotland. It was between the local Macdonells and Macintoshes.
• The **Parallel Roads** high on the hillsides of Glen Roy mark three successive shorelines of a lake that formed at the end of the last ice age.

6

Isle of Skye

Talisker is an Island malt within the Highland classification and the only remaining distillery on the hauntingly beautiful Isle of Skye off the north-west coast of Scotland. It is a hardy environment, both in terms of the landscape – dramatic mountains and great, broad glens scooped out by glaciers – and the people's lifestyle of crofting farms, fishing and distilling. The crofters literally had to fight for basic rights; the riots against the thrall in which they lived brought in, first, armed Government troops to calm things down and, subsequently, the Crofters Act of 1886 which gave some security of tenure.

The island's past is punctuated by Norse invasion and the Lords of the Isles' struggles with Scottish monarchs. There were also clan battles, the Macleods, Macdonalds and Mackinnons continually chafing at each other's territories. The dominant Macleod clan is of mixed Norse and Gaelic descent and Skye place names indicate those parallel influences; the main point of access to the island at Kyleakin is named after a Norse king who tried to make Skye part of his empire, which included Greenland and Iceland.

Above: Sheep are an important part of the economy of Skye. This farmer pauses in front of his flock, with the Storr rock in the background.

Talisker Distillery

Location: **Carbost, Isle of Skye IV47 8SR**
Roads: **On B8009, via A850 and A863 from Sligachan.**
Seasons: **All year, 9.30am - 4.30pm Mon - Fri (July - Aug. Mon - Sat)**
Nov - March 2.00 - 4.30pm Mon - Fri
Group bookings by appointment
Reception centre, exibition and shop
Tel: **01478-640314**

*W*ithin sight of the famous Cuillin Mountains, Talisker distillery sits in the lee of its own hill on the shore of Loch Harport, the buildings pristine white between the vivid green of the slope behind and the slate-blue of the loch water lapping below. It is the hub of the tiny Gaelic-speaking crofting community of Carbost on the loch-side, yet, until recently, English was often heard at the distillery because – how could this be? – the distillery manager was an Englishman! He was also a member of the local mountain-rescue team.

The distillery buildings are built round a central courtyard. The mysterious, pointed twin 'pagoda-head' chimneys that rise above the roofs are vestiges of the old peat-fired ovens, which dried the locally produced malt and gave the whisky its wonderful, distinctively smoky aroma and flavour. Today the malt is peated elsewhere to Talisker's specification, which lies somewhere between the lightness of the Highland malt whiskies on the mainland to the east, and the heaviness of the Islay malts to the south.

This is Clan Macleod territory and over half of the 14 distillery staff are Macleods. When a new lease was negotiated in the 1880s with the chief of the Clan,

Above: The still house at Talisker was re-built in the 1960s, with exact copies of the earlier stills to maintain the character of the spirit.

annual payment was to be £45, plus a 10-gallon cask of 'best-quality' Talisker (duty-free, of course) to be delivered at Michaelmas to Dunvegan Castle.

Talisker was built in 1831 by the MacAskill brothers from Eigg and named after their estate mansion just over the hill. Talisker House was traditionally the residence of the eldest son of the Macleod clan chief and over the centuries saw many distinguished guests. Just beside where the distillery now stands, Boswell and Johnson climbed on to their ponies for the journey over to the House. Sir Walter Scott also visited and Turner found time during a stay to paint Loch Coruisk in one of its more sombre moods.

One of the subsequent owners, J. Anderson, was jailed in 1880 for charging customers for whisky which, he told them, was safely maturing in the Talisker warehouses but which, in fact, did not exist. Talisker was later bought by a partnership, which included Roderick Kemp of Aberdeen who, when he later sold his share, went on to establish the Macallan distillery (*qv*) on Speyside. In 1898 Talisker merged with Dailuaine distillery, also on Speyside, and eventually, in 1925, both were acquired by DCL. In 1900 a pier and tramway were built, making the nightmarish difficulties of hoisting heavy, precious casks over the high side of a coaster from the water below a thing of the past. A dramatic fire in 1960 destroyed the still house, requiring the creation of five exact-copy stills; it must have been a nerve-wracking time during their first distillation-run as everyone waited to see if the nature of the spirit would turn out differently. There was no problem.

In the years prior to the distillery's construction, the MacAskills had played their part in the Highland Clearances, evicting families to make way for Cheviot sheep;

today, by contrast, several of the distillery's staff are crofters and it is quite understood if someone has to slip away for an hour because a cow is calving or a hayrick has blown down. The womenfolk used to weave Harris Tweed cloth part-time at Port na Long at the head of Loch Harport. A century ago, casual workers were paid in tokens which they could spend on fish, bread, oatmeal, and so on at the distillery shop. Some of the tokens are on display today at the reception centre.

Only the manager's house, the offices and the warehouses are pre-1960 buildings. There used to be a waterwheel to supplement steam-engine power and in the 1920s the distillery was lit by acetylene gas lamps. The stills are great onion-shaped kettles, richly gleaming and radiating heat, with ever-narrowing swan-neck tops which gracefully lead their vapours away through the stillroom wall to cool and condense beyond. There are five stills at Talisker, two large ones for the first distillation and three smaller for the final. Their precise size and shape, even the angle at which the swan-neck lies, are vital to the continuing production of spirit with the authentic Talisker signature in aroma and flavour. Talisker used to be triple-distilled but now, like most Scotch malt whisky, it is double-distilled.

Talisker still has worm-pipes – rare in Scotland now – for condensing the vapour that runs off the stills. These spiral tubes of gradually diminishing calibre conduct the vapours down through wooden tubs of water kept constantly cold. Somewhere during the descent, the vapour condenses to liquid which is channelled off to spirit-receivers.

The water descends from Hawk Hill and is very peaty; the burns that run off the hills behind the distillery are rust-red in colour.

The Whisky

Talisker is a highly distinctive whisky with a strong, smoky, peaty flavour because both the malt and the water used to make it are heavily peated. It has had a

distinguished reputation for most of its existence and Robert Louis Stevenson described it as 'king o' drinks' in an 1880 poem. Talisker is usually 45.8% vol. in strength and its optimum bottling age is now deemed to be 10 years. It was formerly bottled at eight years, however, and some very old vintages (1952, 1955) and a 14-year-old are also currently available from independent bottlers

Of interest nearby

Above: Dunvegan Castle, is the seat of the chiefs of the Clan Macleod.

• **Dunvegan Castle** is the oldest continuously inhabited castle in Britain. A lock of Bonnie Prince Charlie's hair, clipped by Flora Macdonald, in its original locket is one of many interesting exhibits. There are white beaches, a seal colony and a shaggy-haired pedigree Highland cattle herd.

• **Colbost Folk Museum** near Dunvegan is a thatched crofthouse and has a richly aromatic peat fire burning most days; there is also a replica of an illicit still.

• The **Clan Donald Centre** at Armadale Castle, seat of the Macdonalds of Sleat, is a combination of clan heartland, Highland heritage exhibition and research centre. It is in a breathtaking coastal location and has 40 acres of restored 19th-century gardens and woodland trails, complete with a countryside ranger service. If you like it, you can stay over in one of the cottages there.

• In a room in the **Royal Hotel** in Portree, Bonnie Prince Charlie parted from Flora Macdonald after the Battle of Culloden to go into exile in France.

• **Kylerhea Otter Haven** has observation hides giving the opportunity to watch otters in the wild. (Across the Sound of Sleat lies **Glenelg**, where lived Gavin Maxwell and the otters described in the book and film *Ring of Bright Water*. It is also the location of two **Brochs**, well-constructed hollow-wall round stone towers which were built by the mysterious Picts.)

• The **Old Skye Crofter Museum** is at Luib; the **Museum of Island Life** at Kilmuir is a group of thatched houses which depict the lifestyle last century.

• The **Quirang** rock formation is most unusual, jagged and fantastic. Viewing it at close quarters on a dark, lowering day can be quite eerie.

• Broadford has a **Serpentarium**, a zoo that specialises in reptiles of many kinds. Skye is a good place to see golden eagles and white-tailed sea eagles

• **Trail End** is really at Kyle of Lochalsh where the car ferry (soon it will be an ugly, bargain-basement bridge) takes you back to the mainland. However, why not close the trail just a little further on down the road from Kyle of Lochalsh at **Eilean Donan Castle**, perched on an islet at the junction of three lochs - Long, Duich and Alsh? It is a beautiful spot, perhaps the most photographed castle in Scotland, and deservedly so.

1

I n d e p e n d e n t   W h i s k y   B o t t l e r s

This wholly inadequate term refers to a very few companies which do much more than just bottle and sell their whisky. One or two of them are recently formed and go back to pre-hi tech methods of preparing their products; others are long-established companies which buy small and large quantities of whisky in cask, often at the earliest fillings stage, and age them the way they see fit in their own warehouses. Unremarkable as these functions may at first seem, their real value is that they make available, in bottle, whiskies in styles and at ages and vintages never offered by the distilleries themselves because they run counter to the main brands marketed by them or because they are too precious to lose from stocks of old whisky.

The range these companies offer is vast, both in depth and breadth. Prices seem high when compared with High Street whiskies but consider what the accumulated costs of a 30-year-old will be, plus the fact that two-thirds of the original quantity will have evaporated over the period that the cask(s) have been warehoused. Moreover, small sizes – including miniatures – are becoming increasingly available so that for a small outlay anyone can now taste, say, 1955 Talisker or even – for a bit more – 1936 Mortlach.

Specialist companies

The following **specialist companies** export all over the world.

• **Praban Na Linne** conducts its business, labels its bottles and prints its letterheads in Gaelic. It prepares 'fior uisge beatha nan Gaidheal' – whisky fit for Highlanders – which features old-fashioned flavours by being unchilled and unfiltered. The business is run at Isleornsay on Skye and you pass their door if you are driving south to Armadale Castle. Their brands are Te Bheag, blended for the Hebrides, and three versions of Poit Dubh, a 12-year-old vatted malt named after the famed sooty 'black pots' in which illicit whisky used to be made, a 12-year-old 46% unchilfiltered version and a 21-year-old at 43%. They also produce a lighter blend called Macnamara

When Te Bheag was exported to Nova Scotia, where Canadian law requires that all products be labelled bilingually (normally English and French), the Liquor Commission accepted its Gaelic and French combination as appropriate to the product. Praban Na Linne is not a large operation and there is little advertising, word-of-mouth recommendation alone bringing in 50 per cent annual growth over the past three years.

• Praban na Linne, Eilean Iarmain, An t-Eilean Sgitheanach (Skye) IV43 8QR, Scotland. Tel: 01471-833266.

• **Gordon & Macphail** may well have the world's largest selection of malt whiskies behind the doors of their deceptively compact shop in Elgin. 'Through the back,' as they say in Scotland, opens out a vast storage, receiving and despatch area where,

you suddenly realise, both casks and cases of bottled whisky are on the move. The darkened warehouses look and smell just like those at the distilleries except that no distillery has anything like the range of names that pass before you as you walk the rows of barrels. The company's beginnings in 1895 were a part of the great whisky boom at that time and today just about anything that can be done with whisky is done by them. The Connoisseurs' Choice range features both well-known and rare distilleries – including many now defunct – at non-mainstream ages and vintages; they also produce a number of other ranges under their own name which are a world away in quality from the customary High Street 'own brands'. From time to time they also experiment using different sorts of casks, e.g. port and brandy casks, to mature their whisky– very unusual and, by all accounts, very interesting.
• Gordon & MacPhail, Boroughbriggs Road, Elgin IV30 1JY, Scotland. Tel: 01343-545111

• **William Cadenhead** was founded in 1842 and specialised not only in malt whisky but in old oak-matured Demerara rum. They must have large telephone bills since the registered office is in Aberdeen, the warehousing in Campbeltown and the main shop in Edinburgh, with a branch in London's Covent Garden. Cadenhead make a point of bottling single casks, preferring to let each display its individuality instead of 'averaging out' over several. It means that no two bottlings, even of identical distillations, are the same. Cadenhead bottle a range of ages from Scotland's malt distilleries past and present not normally available at source and they avoid any filtering or treatments that might remove or alter the whiskies' flavours.
• William Cadenhead, 32 Union Street, Campbeltown, Argyll PA28 6HY, Scotland. Tel: 01586-554258.

• **The Scotch Malt Whisky Society** bottles cask-strength single malts for selling to their 14,000-strong membership around the world. It is based at an old wine warehouse in Leith, the old port of Edinburgh, where there are comfortable club premises for the members and their guests to use. The germ of the idea to form the society was sown in 1983 when a syndicate of friends contributed money totalling £2,500 and set off driving to Glenfarclas distillery to buy a small cask of mature malt whisky which they shared. Now regular bottlings are announced using the society's number system - they are not allowed to use distillery names for copyright reasons. Only single casks are bottled with no averaging out. The society bottles from every distillery in Scotland and offers whiskies that have never been available in single-malt form before. Tastings are held around the UK for members and their guests on a regular basis, private tastings are also catered for.
• The Scotch Malt Whisky Society, The Vaults, 87 Giles Street, Leith, Edinburgh EH6 6BZ, Scotland. Tel: 0131-554 3451.

• **Signatory** is an Edinburgh firm which bottles and markets a range of whiskies in small and large quantities, in cask and bottle, to trade.
• Signatory, 7-8 Eliza Field, Newhaven Rd, Edinburgh EH6 5PY.
Tel: 0131-555 4988.

The Vintage Malt Whisky Co. was established in 1992 and its five brands, **Finlaggan** Single Islay Malt, **Tantallan** Single Highland Malt, **Glenandrew** Single Highland Malt and **Glenalmond** and **Tambowie** vatted malts, are now exported worldwide, with appointed distributors in 12 principal markets. Their range of single cask bottlings is produced under **The Coopers Choice** label and extends to over 20 different malts.
• Vintage Malt Whisky Co., 192 Drymen Road, Bearsden, Glasgow G61 3RW.
Tel/ Fax: 0141-942 9581.

• **Master of Malt** one of Britain's leading mail order suppliers of Single Malt Whiskies, operates The Malt Whisky Association, a subscription society, founded to promote the appreciation of malt whisky. Master of Malt's Specialist Malt Whisky shop and mail-order service is based in Royal Tunbridge Wells, Kent and both members and non-members are most welcome.
• Master of Malt, The Corn Exchange, The Pantiles, Royal Tunbridge Wells, Kent, TN2 5TE. Tel: 01892 513295, Fax: 01892 750487
• The Malt Whisky Association, The Membership Secretary, Largs, Ayrshire, Scotland KA30 8BR. Tel: 01475-676376.

• **The Keepers of the Quaich** is an exclusive, non-profit making and international Society founded by the leading Scotch whisky distillers to honour those around the world who recognise the nobility of Scotch whisky by working, writing or speaking on its behalf.

The organisation includes as members leading representatives of the Scotch whisky industry and those who have contributed to the succesful marketing of Scotch whisky in fifty-eight countries across the world, together with noted Scotch whisky connoisseurs and characters. All have one fundamental link in common – a love of Scotland and Scotch whisky.

The Quaich, the symbol of the society, derives from the Gaelic 'cuach', a drinking bowl
• Keepers of the Quaich, Burke Lodge, 20 London End, Beaconsfield, Bucks. HP9 2JH.
Tel: 01494-670035.
Fax:01494-670230

•*G l o s s a r y   o f   T e r m s*

Age If an age is declared on a label – e.g. 12-year-old – it must be the age of the youngest whisky in the blend.

Blend Normally a mix of pot-still malt whisky and continuous-still grain whisky.

Coffey still see **Continuous still**

Condenser Modern unit attached to still, which cools the alcoholic vapour boiled off during distillation back to liquid form.

Continuous still Distillation unit, which produces uninterrupted flow of spirit for as long as supply of wash is maintained. Also called patent or Coffey still, the latter named after the developer of the original idea.

Dram A glass of whisky. The measure in a bar is traditionally 1/4 gill or 1/5 of a gill in Scotland, and 1/6 of a gill (2.5 cl) elsewhere in the UK.

Feints The unused end-part of a distillation run, which is mostly water.

Fillings Newly distilled spirit, which is filled into oak casks for a minimum of three years' maturation in bonded warehouses.

Foreshots The unused initial part of a distillation run which contains unpalatable esters and higher alcohols. Also called 'heads'. From a run only the middle section is taken; the foreshots and feints (*qv*) are redistilled with the next batch of low wines (*qv*).

Gill see **Dram**

Grain whisky Whisky that is made from cereals other than malted barley.

Grist The precisely ground malt flour immersed in hot water to make sugar-rich mash.

Heads see **Foreshots**

Kiln Room-sized area for drying the malted barley. Smoke from peat or coal fires below rises through a mesh floor and permeates the malt. **Pagoda-head roofs** are the 'chimneys' up which the smoke eventually passes.

Lade A watercourse or millstream.

Low wines The product of the first distillation in the wash still.

Lomond still A variation on the pot still (*qv*), which produces heavier spirit.

Make The make is the whisky or spirit produced by a given distillery.

Malt Barley whose starch content has turned to sugar. Malting is the process of bringing this about on a floor (rare), in a Saladin box (very rare) or in large drums (now standard).

Malt whisky Whisky made exclusively from malted barley by double-distillation in a pot still. It has depth and range of flavour, aroma and complexity unmatched by grain whiskies. Almost without exception malt whiskies vary in detail according to the distilleries that produce them although they can be grouped by broader style characteristics.

Marrying The integration in cask over a period of time of two or more whiskies that have been blended together.

Mash The liquid mixture of grist (*qv*) and hot water.

Middle cut The wholesome heart or core of the distilling run which is separated from feints and foreshots (*qv*) to be aged as whisky.

Nosing Whisky is assessed by sniffing the aromas rather than actually tasting it.

Pagoda head The pyramid-shaped roof with metal terminals above a distillery's malt-kiln from which drying smoke was allowed to escape.

Patent still see **Continuous still**

Peat reek The degree to which a whisky shows smokiness of aroma or taste when a peat fire is used to dry the malt.

Pot still The classic still for double-distilling malt whisky.

Saladin box Low-walled trough with mechanical turners for malting barley. Named after its French inventor.

Sherrywood Oak casks, from Jerez in Spain, that have been used to ferment and/or store sherry. Whisky matured in them acquires richness, sweetness and body. Some whisky firms use only sherrywood, some use none, most prefer a mix of sherry, Bourbon and plain oak casks.

Shiel Wooden spade-like paddle for turning barley on a maltings floor.

Silent season Annual summertime lay-off period in distilleries when production was suspended due to lack of water.

Single malt Pot-still whisky from an individual distillery. Also called a singleton or a self whisky.

Spirit safe Glass-and-brass control box, padlocked by the Excise Officer, which gives sight of spirit running off a still. By its appearance, the stillman decides when to take off the wholesome middle cut of the distillate.

Spirit still The still in which the second and usually final distillation takes place using low wines from the wash still.

Steep Tank for steeping or soaking barley, prior to germinating and malting.

Tails see **Feints**

Uisge beatha Scots Gaelic for *aqua vitae*, 'water of life', from the first part of which the word 'whisky' derives.

Vatted malt A blend of malt whiskies from two or more individual distilleries.

Wash The weak ale created when the wort ferments and which is then distilled in the wash still.

Wash still Still in which the first distillation of the wash takes place to produce low wines.

Whisky or whiskey? Whisky is exclusively Scotch; from anywhere else, it is whiskey.

Worm A coil of copper tubing which is the continuation of the swan-neck top of the spirit still. It passes through a tub of cold water which causes the distillation vapours to condense into liquid.

Wort The liquor made from grist (*qv*) mashed with hot water.

Bibliography

Century Companion to Whiskies, Derek Cooper, Century, 1983
Illicit Scotch, Steve Sillett, Beaver Books, 1965
Jura and George Orwell (no author or publisher credited)
Jura's Heritage, Gordon Wright, Wright, 1991
The Long Road, Peter Youngson, Youngson, 1987
The Making of Scotch Whisky, Michael Moss & John Hume, James & James, 1981
The Malt File, John Lamond, Benedict Books/Malt Whisky Association, 1989
Malt Whisky Almanac, Wallace Milroy, Neil Wilson Publishing, 1992
Malt Whisky Companion, Michael Jackson, Dorling Kindersley, 1989
Michael Jackson's Guide to Single Malt Scotch, Michael Jackson, Running Press, 1991
Mother's Ruin, John Watney, Peter Owen, 1976
Scotch, Sir Robert Bruce Lockhart, Putnam, 1951
Scotch and Water, Neil Wilson, Lochar, 1985
Scotch: its History and Romance, Ross Wilson, David & Charles, 1973
Scotch Whisky, Michael Moss, Chambers, 1991
Scottish Clans & Tartans, Ian Grimble, Hamlyn, 1973
The Scottish Insurrection of 1820, P. Berresford Ellis & Seumas Mac a' Ghobhainn
Scottish Words, Iseabail Macleod, Richard Drew, 1986
The Whisky Distilleries of Scotland and Ireland, Philip Morrice, Harper, 1987
The World Guide to Whiskey, Michael Jackson, Running Press, 1993

Picture Credits